Crown Jewel of Texas

CROWN JEWEL of TEXAS

The Story of San Antonio's River

Lewis F. Fisher

MAVERICK PUBLISHING COMPANY

MAVERICK PUBLISHING COMPANY
P.O. Box 6355, San Antonio, Texas 78209

Publisher's Cataloging-in-Publication Data
(Prepared by Quality Books Inc.)

Fisher, Lewis F.
    Crown jewel of Texas : the story of San Antonio's river / Lewis F. Fisher
    p. cm.
    Includes bibliographical references and index.
    LCCN: 96-79970
    ISBN 0-9651507-1-2
    ISBN (pbk.) 0-9651507-2-0
    1. San Antonio River (Tex.)--History.   2. Paseo del Rio (San Antonio, Tex.)--History.
    I. Title.
F392.S19F57 1997   976.4'12
                           QBI97-40034

06 05 04 03 02 01 00 99 98 97   10 9 8 7 6 5 4 3 2 1

Printed in the United States of America
on acid-free paper

Frontispiece: Looking upstream below the Houston Street bridge, about 1877.
(Photo: The University of Texas at San Antonio Institute of Texan Cultures)

Contents

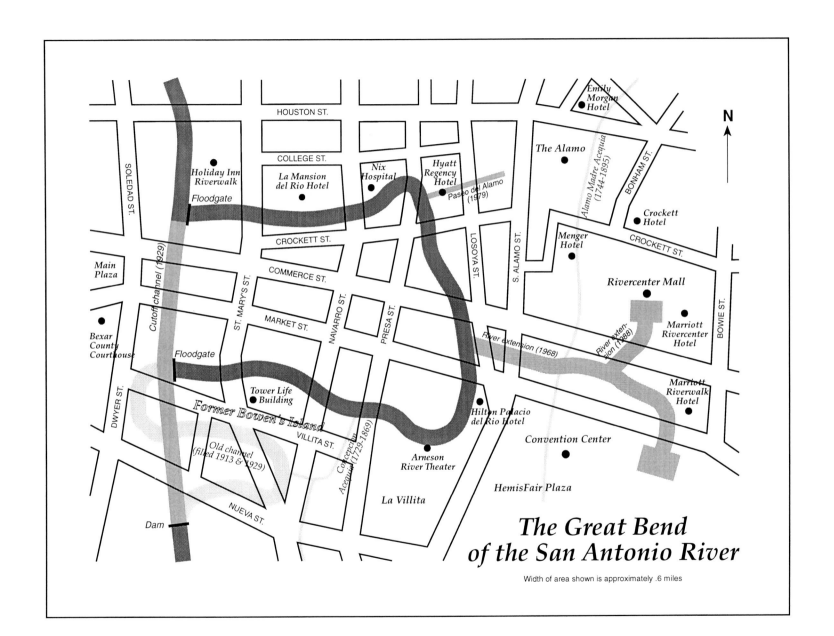

The Great Bend of the San Antonio River

Width of area shown is approximately .6 miles

Preface

Great rivers typically produce great cities. London owes its greatness to the Thames, Paris to the Seine, Cairo to the Nile, New Orleans to the Mississippi.

San Antonio likewise owes much of its stature to the San Antonio River. But unlike most such cities, San Antonio is at the headwaters rather than downstream, and there are no other cities on its river. Past San Antonio, the 180-mile San Antonio River winds through the countryside along a narrow, unnavigable course often overrun with vegetation and choked by debris, emptying unheralded into the deserted San Antonio Bay on the Texas coast of the Gulf of Mexico. This book, then, deals with only the first few, remarkable miles of the San Antonio River.

The impact of this part of the river on San Antonio and the world, not surprisingly, has nothing to do with commercial shipping or industrial might. It has to do instead with an ambiance rarely found along metropolitan rivers, a "linear paradise" created by an intimate River Walk twenty feet below street level along a shaded, meandering stream which in other parts of the country might be dismissed as a creek.

San Antonio's two-mile River Walk has become the most visited attraction in the state of Texas and a world model for sensitive urban development. Its charms have helped vault San Antonio, tourism studies show, into the league of New Orleans and London.

Yet the two centuries of evolution which led to the modern River Walk's creation are only vaguely understood. Virtually nothing has been written of the crucial decades of activity which preceded its ultimate plan, leaving a knowledge vacuum to be filled by myths and fables. But ingenious conjectures cannot, in the long run, substitute for the appeal of the real story.

The eastern leg of the river's Great Bend, looking north.

"Occasionally there is a city . . . in which a stream is appreciated and is regarded as something more than part of a drainage system," wrote a critic in *Architectural Record*. "The average City Council would have built an intercepting sewer, the stream would have disappeared from view and the city would have become as commonplace as any other good hustling, enterprising town. San Antonio saw further . . . , gave it a wider bed than it demanded and then made of this bed an attractive little parkway . . .. In the business center the greatest care has been taken to enhance its attractiveness."

The article appeared in 1919, when the designer of the River Walk as we know it was still a teenager.

Indeed, most efforts now commonly thought to have first arisen in the 1920s began years before. Turning the river into a park was suggested in 1887. Cutting trees along the banks made San Antonians irate in 1904 and brought an immediate municipal river landscaping project. The first Fiesta river parade was held in 1905. Lights were strung along the river in 1907. A leading architect in 1912 proposed a river master plan complete with unique bridges, cafes and boats for tourists, anticipating the Hugman plan—in recent years presumed to be the first—by seventeen years.

Nor was the scheme to drain and pave the Great Bend sprung on an unsuspecting citizenry in the 1920s. It had already been publicly proposed by 1903, and it was the subject of an engineering study in 1911—promoted by businessmen, not by conniving politicians. A city administration, in fact, in 1912 made downtown river beautification a central part of its plan for the city, and the next year landscaped the banks and walled the channel in a project admired by tourists—and architectural critics—for the next twenty-five years.

Too, key elements of the 1920 master flood control plan and opposition to Robert Hugman's River Walk plans, and his dismissal from the project he conceived, have never been quite understood.

Piecing together the story of the evolution and transformation of the San Antonio River resembled an archeological dig. Like the remainder of a ruin poking above the surface, the tantalizing hints led in surprising directions when probed more deeply.

Fortunately, there has been much help along the way. I am particularly grateful to Susan Crane, project administrator at the San Antonio River Authority; Victor Darnell, retired chief engineer of the former Berlin Bridge Company who lives in Kensington, Connecticut; Rebecca Hufstuttler, research associate at the Witte Museum; Jo Myler, manager of the Texana section of the San Antonio Public Library; Craig Likness, assistant librarian at Trinity University's Maddux Library; Carole Prietto, university archivist at Washington University's Olin Library in St. Louis, where the archives of Harland Bartholomew and Associates are kept; Rich Mansfield, corporate librarian for Metcalf and Eddy in Wakefield, Massachusetts; copy editor Sarah Nawrocki; Tom Shelton, the ever resourceful photo archivist at the University of Texas at San Antonio's Institute of Texan Cultures; engineer Douglas Steadman, retired president and chairman of the W.E. Simpson Company Inc., now The Simpson Group; and staffs at the Daughters of the Republic of Texas Library at the Alamo, the Paseo del Rio Association and the San Antonio Conservation Society Library.

Special thanks for reading all or portions of the manuscript and making valuable suggestions go to Bill and Linda Lyons, third-generation owners of the River Walk's pioneering Casa Rio Restaurant; San Antonio River Authority General Manager Fred Pfeiffer and his historian wife, Maria Watson Pfeiffer, plus the River Authority's chief engineer, Steven Ramsey; and architect Boone Powell, of the firm of Ford, Powell and Carson, who has been making significant design contributions to the river for more than thirty years. Valuable, as always, were the insights of my wife, Mary, and of our sons, William and Maverick.

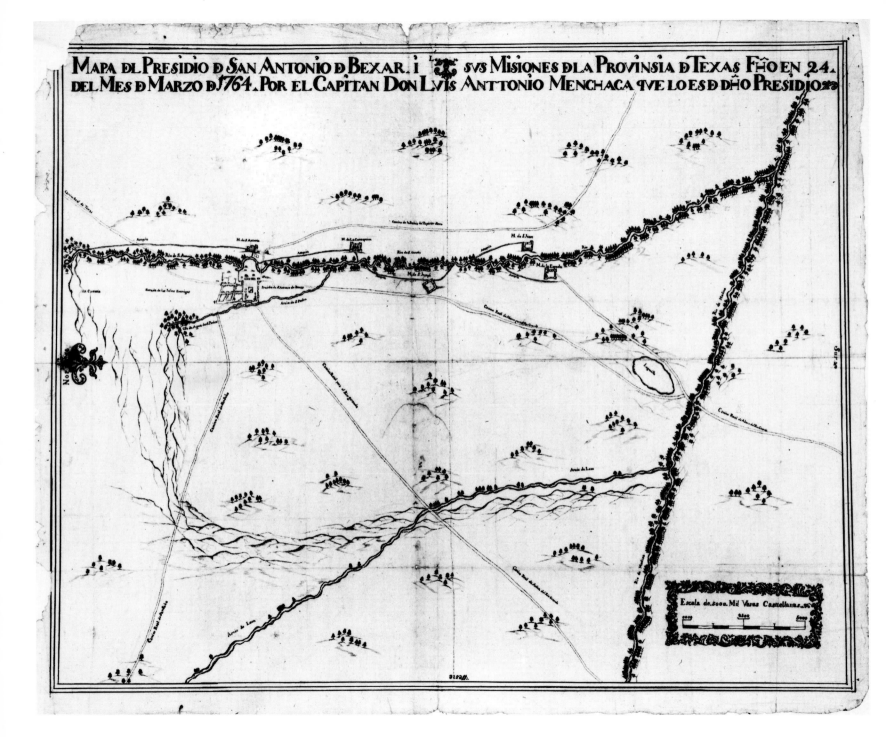

MAPA DL PRESIDIO D SAN ANTONIO D BEXAR. i sus MISIONES DLA PROVINSIA D TEXAS Fhô EN 24. DEL MES D MARZO D 1764. POR EL CAPITAN DON LVIS ANTTONIO MENCHACA QVE LO ES D DhO PRESIDIO

Escala de 500. Mil Varas Castellanas

1. Water for a Spanish Town

No signs point to the source of the San Antonio River. But it doesn't much matter. In the unlikely event that you stumble through underbrush near the suburban University of the Incarnate Word campus and happen upon the Blue Hole, there's little chance of knowing you've found it, much less of getting wet.

Now only when unusually heavy rains return the Edwards Aquifer to its historic heights do the deep springs rise through a narrow shaft of gray-green limestone, its colors giving the waters a bluish cast as they become again, if only briefly, the headwaters of the San Antonio River.

What is designated on National Register of Historic Places maps, if not on site, as the Source of the River Archaeological District is part of a regional complex of small rivers whose waters ran deep before artesian wells lowered the water table at the close of the nineteenth century. Rising from the springs of the Balcones Escarpment to the north, they flow south and east through the brush country and coastal and Rio Grande plains to the Gulf of Mexico.[1]

With little sloping terrain to hurry its flow, the San Antonio River follows an erratic course which led one of its early names to translate into "Drunken Old Man Going Home at Night."

Ten thousand years ago, after the last Ice Age, Paleo-Indian hunter-gatherers were dining on bison, giant horse, mastodon and fish and leaving the bones at a dozen campsites in the Olmos Creek basin and down the San Antonio River through Brackenridge Park. As late as 1928, Oklahoma Indians collected mescal beans in Olmos Basin for peyote ceremonies. They came down an ancient buffalo route once used by the Tonkawa, exiled from the Austin area to Oklahoma before the Civil War.[2]

Opposite page: San Antonio and its five missions are downstream from the river's headwaters, above far left center in this 1764 map looking east. Below the Great Bend and the town is the short San Pedro Creek. At upper right the San Antonio River is joined by the Medina River.

A Spanish-built aqueduct still carries Espada Mission's 1731 acequia across Piedras Creek.

Less than fifty years after Christopher Columbus's first voyage, the Spanish explorer Cabeza de Vaca crossed the San Antonio River in 1535. First to locate its headwaters was a group of Spanish priests and soldiers under Domingo Terán de los Rios and Father Damian Massanet, on their way to the Tejas Indians and the first Spanish missions in East Texas. It was June 13, 1691, the day of St. Anthony of Padua. They named the spot, called Yanaguana by the Indians, San Antonio de Padua.

Scarcely four years had passed since the French explorer LaSalle's ill-fated expedition landed on the Texas coast. The Spanish, unnerved, feared French expansion west from Louisiana into unsettled lands claimed by Spain. The fertile plain below the San Antonio River's headwaters was a logical spot for a stronghold on New Spain's northern frontier.

On May 1, 1718 the Spaniards arrived. Franciscans established the mission San Antonio de Valero, later known as the Alamo, near San Pedro Springs two miles west of the river's headwaters. Four days later, Governor Martín de Alarcón set up a military presidio nearby. Within three years both moved a mile and a half south, where the river, bending and doubling back frequently, allowed homes to cluster along the water, something which could not be done along a straight river. The mission went above the east bank of the river's Great Bend, the presidio to the west beside San Pedro Creek. Between them, Spanish colonists from the Canary Islands in 1731 established the Villa of San Fernando de Bexar.

The Spanish began consolidating their foothold north of the Rio Grande by moving Mission San José y San Miguel de Aguayo in 1720 from East Texas to three miles downstream from San Antonio. Seven years later, three more former East Texas missions moved nearby—Nuestra Señora de la Purísima Concepción de Acuña, San Francisco de la Espada and San Juan Capistrano.

The elements of Spanish San Antonio—a military community, a civilian community and five Catholic mission communities to Christianize the Indians—were in place.

The Spanish were well-prepared for the dry climate they found in South Texas. For centuries in Spain they had worked with irrigation techniques brought from northern Africa by the Moors, who in turn improved on Arab expertise at coaxing a living from semiarid soil. They could separate plots of land and quantities of water into 225 classifications according to degree of soil fertility, slope and suitability for crops.

In 1718 the Spanish began diverting San Antonio River water into a network of acequias—ditches—that served as San Antonio's water system for nearly two hundred years. Headgates or diversion dams in the river—some of rock and brush, others of stone and mortar—kept water high enough to flow into the acequias, which carefully followed the contour of the land. Hollowed-out logs—"canoas"—carried acequias over small depressions or streams. Stone aqueducts were built at major crossings. Water wheels lifted water to higher ground. Wooden headgates in the sides of acequias diverted water into lateral canals.

By 1776, a system of seven acequias was complete. Two carried water through town—the San Pedro Acequia (or Acequia Principal de Bexar) and the Upper Labor Acequia. Five more, built by Indian converts, irrigated mission farmlands—the Alamo Madre, Concepción (or Pajalache), San José, San Juan and Espada acequias. San Antonio's Spanish acequia system is designated a National Historic Civil Engineering Landmark by the American Society of Civil Engineers. The Espada Acequia, in almost continuous use since it was built, is the most complete Spanish irrigation system surviving in the United States.[3]

During Spanish times, San Antonio's 2,000 residents may have made the town the chief settlement in the province of Texas. But far from markets in Mexico to the south and isolated by the French to the east, San Antonio did not prosper, and its appearance was less than pretentious. Its half-dozen substantial buildings were all close to Main and Military plazas. One visitor in 1778 found "fifty-nine houses of stone and mud and seventy-nine of wood, but all poorly built, without any pre-conceived

In San Antonio's early irrigation system, a rock dam in the river diverted water to a waterwheel, which lifted it onto Bowen's Island to irrigate crops.

During the Flood of 1819, water was five feet high in the parish church of San Fernando, built in 1749. The parish priest conducted funeral services for sixteen flood victims.

plan, so that the whole resembles more a poor village than a villa . . . . The streets are tortuous and are filled with mud when it rains."[4]

As San Antonio grew outward along its acequias, the traditional grid pattern of streets around the original plazas was broken as new streets paralleled the water's irregular paths, while lots of uniform width extended property as deep as necessary to reach a water source on acequia, creek or river.

San Antonio may have been nurtured within the folds of a life-giving river's bends, but there came a price. Flooding was bad enough from San Pedro Creek, which drains an area of some three square miles within San Antonio's original city limits; before it joins the San Antonio River to the south, it also receives floodwaters from the twenty-three square miles of the normally dry Apache, Alazan and Martinez creeks' drainage area.

Near its headwaters, however, the San Antonio River catches surges from storms over a dry drainage bed known as Olmos Creek, which drains an area of thirty-four square miles to the north. Major storms over the Olmos Creek basin in particular bode ill for San Antonio.[5]

Such a disaster was first recorded in July 1819. Its cause was given as a "culebra de agua"—a serpent or snake of water, or cloudburst—over Olmos Creek. The rains spawned a torrent unequaled for another century. Raging floodwaters of the San Antonio River joined those of San Pedro Creek to wash away a dozen adobe and stone buildings around Main and Military plazas, according to an account by Antonio Martínez, last governor of Texas under Spain. Waters up to five feet high were reported within the church of San Fernando and even higher on adjacent plazas.

San Fernando's parish priest presided over funerals for sixteen flood victims, ten of them Indian children. Governor Martínez moved the Spanish soldiers from their wrecked barracks on Military Plaza to the higher ground of La Villita.[6]

But flooding was not the only trial for San Antonians as the sun began to set on the Spanish Empire. Many residents fled as Spanish royalists clashed near San Antonio with Mexican revolutionaries. The successful insurgents were in turn challenged by aggrieved Texas immigrants, who lifted a Mexican siege of San Antonio in 1835 despite the loss of men to sharpshooters perched in tall cypresses beside the river. The next year Santa Anna wiped out a Texan garrison at the Alamo. Its defenders dug a well within its walls in case water to their acequia was cut off.

Texans, in turn, defeated Santa Anna at San Jacinto within two months of the fall of the Alamo. But, still endangered by Mexican forays, San Antonio languished under the Republic of Texas, and, at first, after the 1845 annexation of Texas by the United States as well. When the end of the Mexican War in 1848 could finally guarantee San Antonio protection from invasions from south of the border, scarcely 800 persons called the place home.

Future President Rutherford B. Hayes, riding through on horseback shortly afterward at the age of 26, found only an "old, ruined Spanish town."[7]

A cypress on the River Walk is marked for its legendary role during the 1835 Siege of Bexar with this WPA tile work by Ethel Wilson Harris.

BUILT BY

THE BERLIN IRON BRIDGE COMPANY,

BINGHAMTON, N.Y.   EAST BERLIN, CONN.

2. San Antonio Outgrows Its River

Freed from the threat of invasion with the end of the Mexican War, San Antonio blossomed as one of the most colorful cities in America.

Germans, French, Italians, Swiss flocked to the isolated town on the Texas frontier until nearly half its people were foreign-born. Scarcely a decade after the war ended, the influx swelled San Antonio's population tenfold, to 8,000, to the delight of travelers who reveled in the exotic mix.

Frederick Law Olmsted, for one, passing through San Antonio in 1856—two years before he began designing New York City's Central Park—was charmed by its "jumble of races, costumes, languages and buildings." He thought that in the nation only New Orleans could vie with San Antonio in "odd and antiquated foreignness." Olmsted, too, was drawn "irresistibly" to the San Antonio River. He found it "of a rich blue and as pure as crystal, flowing rapidly but noiselessly over pebbles and between reedy banks. One could lean for hours over the bridge rail."[1]

By the end of the century, however, the growth of the city had worn out its river. The flow was no longer swift enough or deep enough for drinking, bathing, boating or carrying off garbage. Its springs drained by artesian wells, cluttered with refuse and shunned as an eyesore and cause of disease, the river faced an uncertain fate.

In the meantime, the party was on.

When the South Texas sun got too hot, San Antonians could jump in their river, unimpeded by swim suits. But by the 1850s, Victorian strictures had to be dealt with. The solution for the modest was to rig a bathhouse in the river to guard bathers from the gaze of others.

Opposite page: Weight of a steamroller demonstrates the strength of the new St. Mary's Street bridge, built in 1890. Symbolism of gold lettering of Mayor Bryan Callaghan's name on plaques overhead on the elegant structure nearly cost the mayor his re-election in the "Letters of Gold" campaign.

Many bathhouses floated on empty, sealed barrels, with frameworks ten feet square sheathed in strips of muslin and wooden floors that could be raised or lowered in the water to keep adults or children at a safe depth. The framework inside held seats and pegs for hanging clothes. Men used the bathhouses early in the morning or late at night, women and children following the afternoon siesta.[2]

Soon there was a bathhouse in the river by the Ursuline Academy for students and resident sisters. A German fraternal group built one by its recreation area on Bowen's Island. A public bathhouse in San Pedro Springs Park took advantage of the natural rock floor around the springs. The first large public bathhouse was put in below the river's Navarro Street/Mill Bridge by a lively entrepreneur named Sammy Hall, who with another kilted Scotsman drew crowds by playing bagpipes and dancing the Highland Fling. But financial ruin drove Hall to suicide as, toward the end of the nineteenth century, the declining river level, increasing pollution and indoor plumbing spelled the end of the bathhouses.[3]

From its headwaters to the end of downtown, the river's elevation dropped thirty-five feet. A half-dozen grist mills were powered by the falling water as were two iron foundries—one of them, the predecessor of Alamo Iron Works, built in 1876 at Market and Presa streets. The dawn-to-dark racket of screeching water wheels and hammering caused the city council to declare "the iron outfit" a public nuisance. It moved outside town to the future location of the Alamodome.[4]

Two breweries opened along the river north of downtown below Brackenridge Park, where doctors found leeches for blood-letting and, during the Civil War, where the Confederacy ran a tannery. A plant to make ice—which resembled frozen snow—opened in 1866 beside the river on Losoya Street, with its largest customer, the Menger Hotel, paying $50 a day for ice service.[5]

Ice forming on the river itself was more rare than a San Antonio snowfall. On one of those occasions it put an end to the ribbing a lieutenant at

Private bathhouses bobbed in the river behind the homes of many San Antonians in the last half of the nineteenth century.

Fort Sam Houston received for bringing ice skates from his previous post in Montana. In February 1899 the river froze for the first time in thirty years, and the young officer was one of the few equipped to enjoy it.[6]

Mineral springs giving birth to resort hotels in southern San Antonio warmed the river, enabling mussels to flourish for five miles below Hot Wells. At the turn of the century, discovery of a freshwater pearl in one mussel led to San Antonio's Pearl Rush, "reminiscent of Klondike days." Piles of shells soon lined that part of the river. Prospectors found up to three dozen valuable pearls a day until all the mussels were gone.[7]

Too, the river offered up fish for the likes of John Blankenship, "the old lone fisherman of San Antonio," whose legendary catches from the Commerce Street bridge included a six-foot eel. Baptismal rites below the Navarro Street/Mill Bridge could be counted on "to bring up a chorus of glorious Hallelujahs following the immersion."[8]

Two entrepreneurs in 1883 planned to add to their two rowboats "a small-sized, low pressure steamboat" to carry twenty-five to fifty passengers from Houston Street around the Great Bend to the Mill Bridge. The steamer *Hilda* was plying the route in 1889. In the 1890s, machinery manufacturer Finis F. Collins ran a steam launch daily, with Sunday trips every twenty minutes. "The water was crowded with other pleasure craft as well," according to one report, "but the steamer lorded it over the whole river." The scene, however, could not last. Though the river was up to fifteen feet deep at some points, it was more shallow in others. Navigation would end when droughts lowered the water.[9]

A bridge helped pedestrians in the 1730s cross the river at Commerce Street between the civilian San Antonio settlement and the Alamo mission. In 1786 Francisco Calaorra received a Spanish land grant on present-day Crockett Street for agreeing to use his boat as a public ferry. But for the most part, early San Antonians simply had to ford the river.[10]

Soon new pedestrian bridges used wooden barrels as pontoons. Floating a foot above the water, they were chained to trees on either side. During rising waters, chains on one side were released so the bridges could be

A dam of rocks diverted water to the iron works at Market and Presa streets until the noisy operation was declared a nuisance and had to move outside town.

Commerce Street got San Antonio's first wagon bridge, shown in 1861.

swept to the other, then pulled back when floodwaters passed. "I always hated to cross this bridge," remembered one San Antonio girl in later life of such a span. "I crawled across it in rainy weather holding on tight on each side. At other times I always stayed right in the middle."[11]

The best wagon ford was at today's southern Navarro Street bridge below the dam, where the river was widest and most shallow. In 1842 the first permanent wagon bridge, "the old red bridge," replaced the Commerce Street ford. When circuses paraded into town, elephants gingerly tested the bridge with their front feet before risking a crossing.[12]

By the Civil War only two bridges—both wooden—crossed the river within city limits, the one connecting East and West Commerce Street and one from East to West Houston Street. By the end of the century there were nearly two dozen, half of wood, the others of iron.

In 1871 the city's first iron bridge, manufactured in St. Louis, had to be shipped by train to New Orleans, by boat to the Texas coast and then overland to be assembled across the river at Houston Street. Arrival of the railroad in 1877 not only ended San Antonio's isolation and sparked rapid growth, it made it easier to get iron bridges. The new supplier was the Berlin Iron Bridge Company of East Berlin, Connecticut.[13]

San Antonio's Berlin bridges became distinctive municipal ornaments. Thanks to the narrow river they were small in scale and did not overwhelm streetscapes. Pairs of unique decorative posts at each end bore the Berlin Bridge Company monogram. The most ornate, at the 1880 Commerce Street bridge, were topped by iron spires in a statement of high Victorian fashion.[14] The Commerce Street bridge reflected San Antonio's cultural diversity with its sign warning riders in three languages—German, English and Spanish—that horses must be walked across. It gained its greatest fame as a setting in O. Henry's short story, "A Fog in Santone."

An iron bridge with overhead trusses high enough to keep from clipping tops of floats in parades was built for St. Mary's Street in 1890. It became a re-election campaign issue for Mayor Bryan Callaghan, whose raised name was lettered in gold paint on overhead plaques at each end.

San Antonio artist Ida Weisselberg Hadra
painted this pastoral scene of the river
flowing beneath the St. Mary's Street
iron footbridge about 1883.

Callaghan survived charges of extravagance, but the race became known
as the "Letters of Gold Campaign."[15]

Without the major riverside industrial zones that sprang up along
larger rivers elsewhere in the nation, the San Antonio River wove a thread
of pastoral beauty through the city.

The baroque southern writer Sidney Lanier observed in 1872 that its
waters were "usually of a lovely milky-green. The stranger, strolling on a
mild sunny day through the streets, often finds himself suddenly on a

The site of the Lewis Mill, which gave the name to the first Mill Bridge, is now a parking lot, while a gently arching span still designated Mill Bridge carries Navarro Street over a quiet section of the River Walk.

bridge, and is half startled with the winding vista of sweet lawns running down to the water, of weeping willows kissing its surface, of summer houses on its banks and of the swift yet smooth-shining stream meandering this way and that, . . . combing the long sea-green locks of a trailing water-grass which sends its waving tresses down the centre of the current for hundreds of feet, . . . murmuring the while with a palpable Spanish lisping which floats up among the rude noises of traffic along the street as it were some dove-voiced Spanish nun out of the convent yonder, praying heaven's mitigation on the wild battle of trade."[16]

Lanier did not, however, portray the dark side of the river—floods, drownings in the whirlpools and deceptively swift undercurrents and periodic epidemics of fever and cholera caused by effluent-polluted water. An epidemic in 1849 killed six hundred people, including Brigadier General William Jenkins Worth, who was camped with his troops near the river's headwaters. Fort Worth was named in his memory.[17]

In 1845, a severe flood caused the city council to urge that the city be moved to higher ground. The mayor thought a dam should be built on Olmos Creek. Seven years later a new mayor brought up the idea again when floodwaters rose eight feet above the river's then normal level, spilling into the streets. But on March 26, 1865, a rain of no greater magnitude than in 1845 caused floodwaters to rise six feet higher than they had twenty years before, flooding streets and causing major property damage. At least three people drowned. A committee of engineers was picked to determine what had caused this flood to be so much worse.[18]

For the first time, official compromises were made between the needs of the mercurial river and those of the growing city. On the advice of the engineers, the Commerce Street wagon bridge was replaced with one lacking its predecessor's mid-river supports. Also, in 1869—after two lesser floods—the obstructing Concepción Acequia diversion dam was removed. The acequia was reopened downstream by connecting it to the Alamo Madre Acequia, but the nearby Nat Lewis Mill, which needed the dam for water power, closed, later reopening with steam power.[19]

In 1866, the polluted river was blamed for yet another cholera epidemic, leaving nearly three hundred dead. There were immediate calls for a modern sanitary underground pipe system to carry drinking water.[20]

But as San Antonio's population ended the decade by growing nearly 50 percent, to more than 12,000, city hall thought it far cheaper to expand the acequia system than replace it with underground pipes. In 1872 a new acequia, the Valley Ditch, was dug southeast from the Alamo Madre Acequia to open new land to development east of town. Although the poorly constructed Valley Ditch was quickly abandoned, a second, the Alazan Ditch, was dug to reach new land on the western edge of the city. Finished in 1876, it headed west and south from the Upper Labor Acequia near San Pedro Springs to join the river southwest of the city.[21]

Trying to serve a fast-growing American city by expanding an aboveground water and sewage system of the type perfected in medieval Spain was simply not, however, going to work. Not only did failure of the Valley Ditch show latter-day San Antonio engineers to be ill-versed in ancient construction techniques, ground contours did not allow gravity-driven acequias to reach many new areas for expansion. Worse, another epidemic of cholera or fever could come at any time.[22]

It was not sanitation but the need for more water for fighting fires that in 1877 finally prompted the city to change directions and sign up with the new San Antonio Water Works Company, formed by immigrant Frenchman Jean Baptiste LaCoste. A pumphouse below the headwaters piped water up a hilltop to the east, where a five-million gallon, eighteen foot-deep reservoir—now preserved, empty, on the grounds of the San Antonio Botanical Center—gave sufficient pressure for the pipes to the city. The company was soon purchased by a group led by banker George W. Brackenridge, who owned the water rights at the headwaters and lived nearby. A second pumphouse was built downstream in 1885.[23]

Then dry weather combined with increasing demands for water to cause the level of the San Antonio River to fall sharply. By late summer in

Bowen's Bend at Bowen's Island provided a contemplative setting in Victorian times.

The traditional lushness of the headwaters of the San Antonio River, shown in this evocative 1880s scene labeled "Silver Fountain," was nearly gone by the close of the nineteenth century.

1887, a drought left the river with "an almost unprecedented lack of water." Water Works officials pleaded with city council—which had set guidelines for water use along the acequias, river and San Pedro Creek in 1830—to limit commercial and industrial use and the watering of lawns and gardens. The council came up with $3,000 to clear away logs and brush to improve the flow. The *San Antonio Light* demanded removal of all dams to allow clear passage of debris and sewage.[24]

An anonymous writer to the *Express* supported the idea, going on to assert that with the acequias closed and dams gone the river would regain "something of its ancient prestige" as "a clear, beautiful stream." It could even become a park. "Its banks could be converted into flower beds, and pleasure boats [could] afford recreation to hundreds . . . . Many of our citizens are prone to look entirely upon the utility side of every question and the river as an ornament would be likely to excite ridicule, but . . . our river would be the crown jewel of Texas."[25]

Most citizens at the time did stick to the utility side of the question. Despairing of more surface river water, George Brackenridge tried drilling artesian wells into the Edwards Aquifer, a 2,100-square-mile underground reservoir then just beginning to be tapped by deep wells.

In 1891, where Market Street meets the river, at 890 feet Brackenridge's drillers hit water with such pressure that it blew out rocks "as large as a man's head" and gushed twenty feet into the air. Nearby, seven more wells were drilled and a pumping facility was built.[26]

The San Antonio Water Works Company began depending not on the headwaters' springs but on the artesian wells, which lowered the springs and the river even further. At last the Spanish acequias were recognized as having become totally obsolete. They fell into disuse, although farmers far downstream organized private cooperatives to maintain the Espada and San Juan acequias. The municipal office of Ditch Commissioner was abolished in 1899.[27]

George Brackenridge no longer needed to keep a close eye on the once lush area around the headwaters. He gave 320 acres of riverside land below his estate to the City of San Antonio for Brackenridge Park. In 1897 he sold the estate to the Sisters of Charity of the Incarnate Word for their motherhouse and academy. A rock dam at the headwaters had created a lake deep enough for flat-bottomed rowboats, but it could not be sustained by the weakened springs.[28]

Wrote Brackenridge to a friend: "I have seen this bold, bubbling, laughing river dwindle and fade away. This river is my child and it is dying, and I cannot stay here to see its last gasps . . . . I must go."[29]

A pumphouse built in 1878 in present-day Brackenridge Park helped lower the river level as it sent water to a new reservoir.

3. A Centerpiece for Urban Reform

As the fast-growing city's demand for more water continued to sap the river's strength, by 1900 all it took was a sustained drought for the headwaters to dry up altogether. Only runoff from wells of two breweries south of Brackenridge Park kept any water in the river downtown.

The bathhouses were gone, the swimming holes were too shallow and boating at the headwaters was only a memory. With little flow to carry off garbage and refuse accumulating on the muddy bottom, city sanitary inspectors ordered those piping wastewater into the river to stop.[1]

Shocked by their beloved stream's decline from a rushing river to a sluggish trickle through slime and silt, San Antonians came to the rescue.

Within the next ten years, tree cutting along the river was protested, new trees were planted, two Fiesta river parades were held, the river was lighted for a Venetian Carnival and auxiliary pumping refilled the stream when it next went dry. Businessmen held plans to fill the river in abeyance as two leading architects came up with plans for its development. A reform administration sweeping into city hall made the river a focal point for municipal improvements and launched the river's first major beautification project, praised in at least one national magazine.

Despite a wet season that began in November 1902 and culminated in a flood three months later, within a year the river was drying up once again. San Antonians recalled stories passed down from Spanish times, when severe droughts threatened the flow through the acequias. Families then assembled at assigned places and, "with all manner of agricultural and farm implements known in that day," scraped away accumulations of mud down to the gravel riverbed. Springs once more bubbled up from

Opposite page: In 1912, architect Harvey Page proposed the first technical master plan to improve the San Antonio River. This cross-section shows how sloping concrete slabs would interlock for a uniform riverbed, enhancing tourist appeal.

Indiscriminate cutting of dense growth along the river in 1904 brought an uproar from citizens concerned with preserving the river's natural beauty.

the bottom. And so, in 1904, the fire department gave the riverbed a scouring. The river gradually rose, whether from the cleaning or from new rains. Weekend boaters again dotted the river, its banks overhung with "boughs, cresses and ferns."[2]

The street department was sent to help by removing some trees along the banks. But in the summer of 1904 a crew made the misstep of cutting down two "magnificent" willow trees. In protest, the young Civic Improvement Association delivered to council chambers "a full hundred citizens of the staid, sober and substantial kind that does not venture out except upon occasions of real merit."

A series of indignant speakers took the street commissioner to task for not obeying council instructions following an earlier incident. Mayor Pro Tem Vories Brown satisfied the crowd by reassigning the job to Park Commissioner Ludwig Mahncke and announcing that new grass and trees would be planted beside the river. The Civic Improvement Association thanked Brown and also the press, "for its efforts in behalf of preserving the river which has made San Antonio noted abroad."[3]

City officials, "uniformly favorable to the river," promised "to beautify the stream and protect it in every manner possible." Penalties were set for unauthorized cutting of riverside trees and shrubs. Authorities prepared to defend the city's river property line against encroachments.[4]

Next the river helped launch San Antonio's Fiesta, which traditionally began with a masked king's arrival at a railroad station. But on the evening of April 24, 1905, the king arrived for the first time on the river. Waters from heavy rains subsided in time to permit a safe voyage for the flower-bedecked, torchlit flotilla, its royal barge decorated in silver and gold. In a scene "not unlike the ancient glories of the Bosphorous in the day of the Caesars," a steady blast of trumpets heralded the fleet's arrival at the landing along the beautified Tobin Terrace below Crockett Street, between St. Mary's and Navarro streets. Crowds cheered as the king was greeted by the commodore of the "Alamo Yacht Club" and ascended with his entourage to the street for an illuminated parade.[5]

The next month, the Tobin Terrace landing was the setting for a Memorial Day service organized by the Women's Relief Corps in honor of deceased sailors. "At the proper time during the exercises," a newspaper reported, "a number of children led by a little boy holding an American flag aloft stepped on a floating barge. As the barge glided gently along with the rippling current, the children showered flowers upon the water, and those along the bank did likewise."[6]

A riverside "Carnival of Venice" planned to open Fiesta two years later was delayed for three nights when a cloudburst washed out a temporary dam built to raise the level of the dwindling river for another boat parade. The dam was rebuilt, and on April 19, 1907, thousands gathered on bridges and banks to watch the king come down the river. Strings of colored lights criss-crossed the river and glowed in its trees from Houston Street to the Navarro Street/Mill Bridge.

Each of the dozen skiffs was lit with strings of Japanese lanterns and carried costumed "Indians and their squaws, . . . very grotesque" in the light of their torches. A searchlight in the lead boat played on the crowds and the river. As the barge of the masked king —later revealed to be John H. Kirkpatrick—drew up to the Tobin Terrace landing, the other boats passed in review, then circled back up to Houston Street. A band played "See the Conquering Hero Comes," fireworks on the riverbank went off "and the crowd shouted itself hoarse."[7]

Evidently due to the river's unpredictable level, boat parades were not held again for nearly three decades. Yet the river was not ignored. For Fiesta in 1910, "many thousands of tri-colored electric globes" were strung across and along its banks in the business district by electrician Martin Wright. As its float in the parade the Civic Improvement League built a twenty-foot canoe, with "rowers" representing the old and the new. On the canoe was a banner emblazoned, "What the Civic Improvement League is going to do with the San Antonio River."[8]

True to a headline declaring "Public Wants River To Receive First Attention," the Civic Improvement League began its efforts to beautify

Children on a barge threw flowers on the river in memory of deceased sailors during Memorial Day ceremonies in 1905.

Beautifying such dismal stretches of the river as this one west of the St. Mary's Street bridge was a challenge for the new Civic Improvement League in 1910.

San Antonio by beautifying three sections of the river downtown by planting grass, flowers and shrubs. An island below the Navarro Street-Mill Bridge was to become a garden of roses and ferns. The riverbed was to be smoothed to a uniform depth to make its flow more even. Public baths were to make up for the loss of a deep river.[9]

During the dry summer of 1910, however, the river slowed to a trickle once again. Farmers along the two surviving acequias south of town fell to quarreling over what little water there was. It took a court to decide that since the Spanish water grant for the San Juan Acequia was dated one day before that for the Espada Acequia, 60 percent of the river's water would be diverted to San Juan and 40 percent to Espada.[10]

But something, clearly, had to be done about the entire river situation.

Early in 1911, the *San Antonio Light* contrasted a photo of overgrown riverbanks south of Houston Street with a rendering of the same scene by London-born architect Alfred Giles, showing boats being rowed on a channeled river as pedestrians passed on walkways on either side. Thought the *Light*: "A comparison of the two pictures . . . shows in a striking manner how easily one of the ugliest spots in the city can be converted into one of the most attractive."[11]

But that summer the river went totally dry not only at its headwaters but all the way to the city itself. Deep cracks opened in the riverbed's dried mud. Wells used by the two breweries at the northern edge of the city kept some water flowing through downtown, but the river between Houston and Commerce streets remained branded one of the worst-looking areas of the city. "Day by day it offends the eyes of thousands of people as they cross the Houston Street bridge," complained the *Light*.[12]

Then an alternative to beautification was studied, ominously, by several businessmen.

The flood in 1903 had prompted architect Francis Bowen to raise an issue he said was already being discussed: to cut a new river channel straight through the heart of the city. This would not only improve runoff, "it would do away with a circuitous dirty river as well . . . and give a great deal of space to some better purpose." As time passed, the idea grew that the river, by then "little more than a creek," should be "closed up and transformed into a driveway." Finally, in the summer of 1911, a group of downtown businessmen hungry for new space for development commissioned a study of their solution by engineer Willard Simpson.[13]

Simpson concluded that most of the river downtown could indeed be filled in. The river and its floodwaters could be carried through an underground conduit from Travis Street past Nueva Street. The ugly stretch between Houston and Commerce streets would disappear, as would the entire Great Bend. Nine high-maintenance bridges, six of them across the Great Bend, could be eliminated. A strip of land some seventy feet wide and more than a mile long would become prime real estate.[14]

In 1911, enthusiasm for improving the San Antonio River, as in Alfred Giles's plan for a river walk between Houston and Commerce streets, apparently caused businessmen to put their scheme to drain and fill the Great Bend on hold.

No matter whether they were seeking to bury the river or trying to save it, San Antonians had to contend with the "cloud of Callaghanism," the shadow of the political machine of longtime Mayor Bryan Callaghan II. Saying that the city's growth would slow, Callaghan kept taxes low and had few bond elections. If San Antonians wanted more paved streets or new gas and sewer lines or other amenities, they could come up with ways to pay for them privately. City hall might be falling behind in providing basic services, but it was not going to move forward any faster.[15]

More and more San Antonians, however, believed such an attitude had no place in what was, after all, the largest city in the largest state. Progressive San Antonians thought their city—which had grown in a decade by more than 80 percent, to 100,000 by 1910—should act in a manner befitting its rank and take its place among the leading cities of America by embracing the City Beautiful movement. Kansas City had, Denver, Seattle, as had even that upstart metropolis to the north, Dallas. No simple clean-up, fix-up effort, City Beautiful reform combined wide-ranging civic improvement activism and environmental awareness with political reform, and developed modern principles of city planning.[16]

A scourge of billboards plagued the area of the Commerce Street iron bridge—with its unique spires—and many other sites as well, until reformers got an ordinance passed in 1911.

As San Antonians became City Beautiful converts, they created perhaps the most broadly based reform movement in San Antonio's history.

San Antonio suffered, as did other cities at the time, from unpaved streets, an inadequate sewer system and from undirected growth. Moreover, progressive San Antonians were appalled at the condition of their river. Improving the river became an essential focus of their efforts.

With no help coming from city hall, San Antonians, following City Beautiful precepts, in 1909 organized a political reform committee, and then a Commission Government League seeking to change the city charter to replace ward-based aldermen with at-large commissioners, each assigned specific urban services. In the heated campaign that followed, reformers pledged to "knock into smithereens the cloud of Callaghanism which has hovered over San Antonio for the past quarter of a century."[17]

A record 80 percent of San Antonio voters turned out for the charter election in February 1911. Of 14,000 votes cast, the proposed charter was defeated by a margin of only 160.[18]

As San Antonio's continued to grow, numerous specific improvement groups arose. A Playground and Recreation Association raised funds to purchase and equip a Buena Vista Street plot as a playground. A Civic Improvement Art League was formed. A Coliseum League began raising funds for a 12,000-seat coliseum. The Woman's Club and the Chamber of Commerce proposed a coordinating Civic Improvement Federation "to promote the health and beauty of the city." The Alamo Film Company planned a movie to show even "in other countries, . . . giving the widest publicity to the general plan for keeping San Antonio sanitary and attractive." The City Federation of Women's Clubs gained a measure of success against "the billboard nuisance," persuading city council to pass an ordinance curtailing billboards.[19]

It was the river, however, which drew reformers' greatest attention. As the *Express* put it: "Few cities possess so great a natural asset as a winding, tree-shaded stream such as the San Antonio River. Its sinuous course through the city . . . elicits the admiration of visitors, even though the stream has dwindled to a sluggish current running through neglected banks over a riverbed covered with slime and silt." But with "its banks beautified, dredged and made a clear, swift stream as it was in 'the old days,' it would be the chief factor in the San Antonio Beautiful."[20]

The outpouring of public support for a beautified river apparently caused businessmen wishing to bury the river downtown to shelve their study for another nine years.

On the evening of September 26, 1911, three dozen citizens gathered at the Chamber of Commerce headquarters to form the San Antonio River Improvement Association. Banker Thomas L. Conroy declared there had to be a way to revive the river, "and it must be found." The president of the City Federation of Women's Clubs, Mrs. M.J. Bliem, promised the help of her constituency in beautifying the river. The new River Improvement Association President, hotelier M.B. Hutchins, assured city council that his group had "no intent to inject politics into the movement"; members simply wanted to show that people were "deeply interested" in seeing water back in the river and having the river cleaned and beautified.[21]

Such an assurance was sufficient for Mayor Callaghan to approve installation of a fifty-horsepower pump at an abandoned artesian well by the river at the northern end of Brackenridge Park—at no cost to the city. The mayor refused to allow the city to pay for a shelter over the pump and vetoed a $500 prize for plans for a series of dams, flood gates and flushing devices. He did authorize city laborers to clear fallen trees and undergrowth from the dry upper riverbed.[22]

From the new water level six feet below the surface, 500 gallons a minute were soon being pumped into the riverbed, then 1,000 gallons, then 1,500. The pump ran for two and a half hours at a stretch, then ten, then twenty. Curious San Antonians flocked to the site as water slowly filled the deep holes and cracks. Long-dormant springs began to reappear. But the millions of gallons were not reaching the river's downtown banks nor even, a half mile north of Josephine Street, "Page's fishing

Shallow stretches of the river gave boys the opportunity to stage money-making buggy washings, as this one in 1917. Water also expanded the wooden wheels, keeping them tight to their metal rims.

As chairman of the new City Plan Committee, Atlee B. Ayres made river beautification a top priority.

hole," which nevertheless suddenly brimmed with "beautiful blue water" once again.[23]

Miles downstream, farmers who had given up their crops for lost found water inexplicably filling the two old mission acequias; it "brought out the greenness and changed the appearance of everything in this valley." A reporter dispatched to the scene found workers too busy harvesting to speculate on whether the unexpected water surfaced from some unknown underground channel starting near Brackenridge Park.[24]

But other than getting some water in the river, reformers had little luck with a recalcitrant city hall. City council defeated a street-paving ordinance by a vote of seven to five. A plan to dredge the river and remove accumulated refuse met with familiar equivocations, as did proposals for the city to pay for continued pumping and to dam the river and make a park along its banks within city limits.[25]

Then suddenly, in mid-1912, halfway through his seventh term in office, Mayor Bryan Callaghan died. Six weeks later, political reform candidate Augustus H. Jones, a rancher and financial backer of the new St. Anthony Hotel, was inaugurated mayor. The old political machine was out. The Citizen's League was in.

Mayor Jones wasted little time. Less than two weeks after his inauguration, he took what one newspaper termed "the first big step to make this a City Beautiful and a Greater San Antonio"—appointment of a City Plan Committee. Boston, Chicago, Denver, Cleveland and several dozen other cities already had formal plans. Why shouldn't San Antonio? "San Antonio can be made the most beautiful place in the country," Jones believed, "and when that is done there will be a rush of homeseekers from all parts of the country."[26]

To chair the City Plan Committee the mayor picked rising young architect Atlee B. Ayres. Reformer Thomas Conroy was made vice chairman. Its members agreed with Civic Improvement League director T.N. Smith, who declared, "No complete plan could be adopted that would not include the preserving and beautifying of the river. The river cannot be beautiful through the business district if buildings line its course to the water's edge . . . . No city plan will be complete that does not include space along its banks for flowers, colonnades, pergolas, etc. in addition to the parks and plazas we now have [elsewhere]."[27]

Ayres made river beautification his top priority, along with upgrading facilities and rescuing dying trees and foliage in Brackenridge and San Pedro parks. The day after his appointment he declared the river's width should be made uniform with walls, its banks terraced and planted with flowers and trees. There were to be footpaths, lighted at night, along the river. Concrete bridges "built along classic lines" should replace high-maintenance bridges. The project would be like those "carried out with a wonderfully gratifying effect throughout Europe."[28]

Four days later, the City Plan Committee unanimously endorsed a plan unveiled by one of its members—another leading San Antonio architect, Washington, D.C. born Harvey L. Page.

Harvey Page, it turned out, had been pondering the subject for some time. Basic to his plan were interlocking, "indestructible" reinforced concrete slabs four inches thick, four feet in width and eight feet in height and sloping toward the channel's center, to create a faster midstream current to speed floodwaters through the city. They would line the river for thirteen miles. Page estimated they could be built on site and hoisted into place for no more than the cost of a sidewalk of similar size. Dams to preserve the water level would include small locks for dredgeboats, which would maintain "an absolutely sanitary stream."

Also, streets crossing the river would get decorative concrete bridges. Numerous benches would turn the banks into "a vast park," while "at night myriads of electric bulbs will shine from the trees while Mexicans dressed in the garb of Aztec Indians will paddle canoes, filled with tourists . . . . [and] stopping at picturesque mission landings for refreshments. . . . Firefly lights playing in the trees and in the shrubbery along the banks, with here and there a moonlight effect from a larger lamp, . . .

In the flurry of plans following formation of the River Improvement Association, James N. Converse rendered this proposal for Alvah Davis's campaign for a river walk south of the Houston Street bridge.

Under a reform administration, city workmen in 1913 began a long-awaited beautification project along the river.

[will] make the San Antonio River a bit of fairyland and unlike anything in the world."[29]

Page estimated his plan would cost no more than $1 million, to be repaid by canoe concession fees. It would not only relieve flooding, it would "do away with all chances of breeding disease." The value of private riverside property would rise. Predicted one newspaper: "The San Antonio River may again be the pride of all San Antonio, and this stream may be made the most unique in the United States . . . . The famous canal of Venice will not compare with the San Antonio River, and tourists will come thousands of miles to see this city and this stream."[30] One headline writer was sufficiently impressed to write, "City Beautiful In Sight."

Indeed, in the first months of the Jones administration it was hard not to get carried away with enthusiasm over what seemed to lie just ahead. T.N. Smith took charge of a committee to reform the structure of city government. City council, instead of quibbling over costs, summarily appropriated $1,000 to put a pump back beside the river in Brackenridge Park, while Harvey Page and two others went to work on beautifying the river below the Navarro Street/Mill Bridge. To prepare a master plan, the City Plan Committee recommended hiring George E. Kessler of Kansas City, one of the nation's leading planners and City Beautiful advocates, then at work on plans for Kansas City and Dallas. A $6,000 public fund was set up to pay his fee. Mayor Jones contributed the first $50.[31]

True to his promises, soon after taking office Augustus Jones authorized the first major beautification project on the San Antonio River. As River Commissioner he appointed George Surkey, a Missouri-born one-time railroad fireman, engineer and roundhouse foreman who became a city councilman before going into real estate. With city money, Surkey constructed a modified version of Harvey Page's plan. Low concrete-covered rock walls—dubbed the "Surkey Sea Walls"—established a uniform width for the downtown river channel. Next came sodding and planting. Surkey sought a new artesian well to double the river's flow.[32]

Then the city considered straightening the river at opposite ends of downtown. Where the southern leg of the Great Bend doubled back to define Bowen's Island, Lafayette Ward got permission to dig a cutoff channel to eliminate part of the switchback. The old section would remain filled with water as "a large natatorium and wading pool" for the Sans Souci Amusement Park, to be "one of the south's most elaborate and best-equipped." The erstwhile riverbank would become a beach.[33]

No agreement, however, was reached on Paul Knittel's plan to shorten a circuitous bend and gain title to the former riverbed just north of downtown. Soon the favored site for the coliseum was changed from the proposed—but never built—Bowen's Island amusement complex to beside the circuitous northern bend, where, when the bend was finally straightened, Municipal Auditorium would be constructed.[34] Knittel also dared to suggest eliminating the Great Bend, not with a buried conduit but with a canal following the course planned for the conduit. Said he: "Just think of the improvement that would follow the filling up of the riverbed all round that long sweep that channel now follows."[35]

Less than eight months after it began, the Augustus Jones administration ended with the sudden death of the 53-year-old mayor. But Camelot did not come to a close. Mayor Pro Tem Albert Steves left office nearly two months later having advocated continuing beautification of the river and building a dam on Olmos Creek for flood contol and a reservoir.[36]

The Citizen's League made a clean sweep in the next election, winning every council seat in a victory seen as a mandate for the long-awaited bond issue. Before he took office the new mayor, former district attorney Clinton L. Brown, personally inspected municipal improvements in Kansas City, Dallas and Fort Worth. Soon a $3.5 million bond issue passed, providing funds for new bridges over the river. But as River Commissioner George Surkey continued work on his "sea walls," his new budget request was cut by nearly half. When he ran out of stone in mid-1913 he recycled rocks from buildings razed in the widening of Commerce Street.[37]

River Commissioner George Surkey directed the river's first major beautification project.

At dedication ceremonies for the Commerce Street widening project in 1914, electric lights strung by the Rotary Club of San Antonio were switched on above the newly improved river channel.

During the widening, Commerce Street's landmark iron bridge with its four spires was moved downstream to make way for a wider bridge of concrete. Relics found in the river during excavations for the new bridge included a cannon ball, bayonet, bullet molds and part of a brass cannon of the type used at the Alamo.[38]

The late Augustus Jones was not forgotten. The new bridge was named Jones Bridge. With help from the Italian-born sculptor Pompeo Coppini, the bridge incorporated street-level alcoves on either side and added concrete ornamentation visible from the riverbanks. For the northern alcove, Coppini designed a statue of a seated Augustus Jones to be cast in bronze and placed on a granite pedestal. For the southern alcove,

Coppini's student Waldine Tauch designed in imitation granite a figure of an Indian wearing a headdress and holding in each hand "two fountains of bubbling water," representing the gift of the river below to those who came later. Although the statue of Jones was never cast, "The First Inhabitant" has become one of the city's most familiar pieces of public art.[39]

On the evening of November 21, 1914, nearly 50,000 San Antonians gathered in the streets around the new Jones Bridge for the highlight of the day-long Commerce Street project dedication. Celebrants cheered as Mayor Brown recognized River Commissioner George Surkey for his work. The touch of a switch lit up the newly beautified riverbanks from Market Street a block south and on north past Commerce Street around the Great Bend and beyond to the Houston Street bridge. Stringing lights across the river was a project of the two-year-old Rotary Club of San Antonio.[40]

Momentum for change continued, with mixed results. The commission form of city government was adopted, but a city planner was not hired. An irrigation system in San Pedro Park saved its ancient trees, and a new pump was installed to start its springs flowing again and raise its lake to the old level. But the city's Boulevard Committee was unsuccessful with its San Pedro Creek beautification plan, which included a San Pedro Boulevard along the banks.[41]

Nevertheless, the face of San Antonio and its river had been decisively changed for the better, and the work on the river inspired plans to improve it even more. In 1915, real estate man Alvah B. Davis got property owners to consider a plan illustrated by draftsman James N. Converse for twelve-foot-wide lighted sidewalks on both sides of the river between Houston and St. Mary's streets, in the prescient belief that a river promenade would make river-level frontage at least as valuable as frontage on the streets above.[42]

But a series of disastrous floods that began in the fall of 1913 sent the clear message that before any such projects took place, San Antonio had to be made safe from its river.

The new Commerce Street bridge got "The First Inhabitant," but no statue of the late Mayor Jones.

ABOVE: LEWIS F. FISHER
BELOW: POMPEO COPPINI, *FROM DAWN TO SUNSET*

4. Six Floods in Nine Years

Precisely two years after drought-plagued San Antonians for the first time pumped water into the dry bed of the San Antonio River, nature made one of its overcompensations.

On the afternoon of October 1, 1913, abnormally heavy rains turned the river into "a surging mass of muddy waters" far beyond its banks up to waist level in downtown streets. Four people drowned, all members of one family fleeing rising water at their home near San José mission. There were numerous close calls. Bridges were damaged, and businesses suffered losses totalling $250,000. Train service to San Antonio was halted as flooding extended through East Texas to Louisiana.[1]

Calls by Mayor Clinton Brown and other city officials for a dam on Olmos Creek north of the city had hardly died down when on December 4 more heavy rains over the Olmos sent the river on an even greater rampage. This time San Antonians were better prepared. There was no loss of life in the city, although more than fifty persons died from flooding elsewhere in the state. Several bridges in the county were swept away, but losses downtown did not exceed $50,000. When trains held up by high water could not deliver regular newsprint, the *Express* was printed on the pink paper normally reserved for sports sections. An engineer designing the city's long-needed sewer system, Samuel M. Gray of Providence, Rhode Island, was asked to also make a report on the river.[2]

Soon other engineers were volunteering ideas. One brought up an old notion that a channel be dug from the headwaters east to Salado Creek to send floodwaters around the city. Another favored "a wall pierced by openings" between low bluffs across the eastern end of what became Hildebrand Avenue. A third, E.A. Giraud, thought the idea of diverting

Opposite page: Soldiers guarding against looting after the 1921 flood kept their feet dry by standing on islands of mesquite paving blocks not swept away. Floodwaters coursing down this stretch of North St. Mary's Street toward Houston Street reached a depth of twelve feet.

Workmen north of the Pecan Street bridge in 1920 stand beside a lumber retaining wall being built to combat the river's flooding.

floodwaters to Salado Creek not only unnecessary but impractical, since it would require a deep half-mile cut from Olmos Basin and then a tunnel more than a mile long to reach the Salado. Straightening the river through the city he thought would be "almost impracticable" financially and would "destroy the natural beauty of the river." Giraud believed the entire problem could be solved instead with "a monolithic concrete dam" near the mouth of Olmos Basin, between two high bluffs northeast of the river's headwaters. Recent City Engineer Aaron Pancoast believed that proposal "the best by far of any plan heretofore advocated."[3]

There were also many ideas about how to combat overflows downtown. Encroachments and obstructions should be removed, streets raised, bridges made higher so they would not become dams. The engineer who wanted floodwaters diverted to Salado Creek declared "unequivocally upon his record as a drainage engineer" that any idea of straightening the river channel "is idle talk and out of the question." The channel was "a product of nature." Tampering with it would only make matters worse.[4]

River Commissioner George Surkey favored an underground spillway to carry overflow from the river at Navarro Street beneath downtown to empty near Nueva Street. Fire Chief Phil Wright thought there should be two underground spillways, one beneath St. Mary's Street and the other beneath Navarro—then Romana—Street.[5]

As time passed, the urgency of a solution faded but did not disappear. In 1917 the city engineer, Norwegian immigrant Hans R.F. Helland, came up with a plan to build a half mile of twenty-two-foot-high retaining walls of pine planks and cypress pilings between Navarro and Houston streets. Parks and Sanitation Commissioner Ray Lambert believed climbing vines would turn the walls into "an object of beauty." Suction pumps would remove silt to make the channel a uniform width. But bids came in too high, and the city did not build the walls.[6]

Under the supervision of River Engineer Albert Marbach, in 1920 lumber walls were built for a shorter distance—between Travis and Pecan streets—apparently with funds approved in a wide-ranging 1919 bond issue, which included $200,000 for "widening, deepening, altering and changing" the river channel to prevent flooding. The funds were also to finance a cutoff channel to eliminate a convoluted bend north of Navarro Street. Seven years earlier a Coliseum League unsuccessfully tried raising funds for a coliseum inside the bend. Now the city saw the site's potential for an auditorium if the bend were eliminated.[7]

But given the welter of proposals in recent years, city commissioners realized they needed top-flight advice before making serious changes to the river. On June 9, 1920, the city signed up with the nationally recognized Boston firm of Metcalf and Eddy. Partner Leonard Metcalf, a Galveston native, knew San Antonio well, having done four technical reports for the San Antonio Water Works Company since 1908.

Two streams threatened downtown San Antonio in 1920—the river, seen above Houston Street where Jazz-Land overlooked the landscaped channel, and San Pedro Creek, seen in its narrow channel north of Commerce Street.

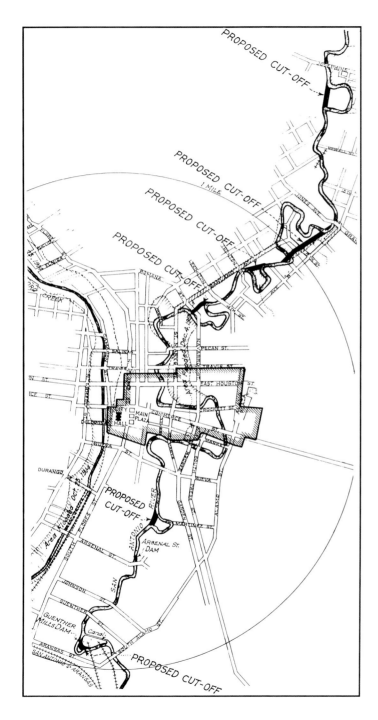

Led by Metcalf and his associate Charles W. Sherman, the firm spent nearly six months studying local flood conditions and meeting with officials from Mayor Sam C. Bell to River Engineer Albert Marbach to Citizens Flood Prevention Committee President L.J. Hart. Data on the river and its tributaries was "too limited to enable safe conclusions," so the engineers pored over U.S. Weather Bureau and U.S. Geological Survey data. They walked "practically every foot" of the river through the city as well as the length of San Pedro Creek, and explored the usually dry drainage basins of Alazan, Martinez and Apache creeks.[8]

On December 6, 1920, the city was presented a 348-page report, including supporting documentation. Included were thirty tables of data and sixty diagrams, drawings and maps showing existing conditions and recommended improvements.

Metcalf and Eddy concluded that the narrow width of the river, lack of a dam and riverbed obstructions would continue to cause periodic flooding if nothing was done. Maintenance indeed may have become more regular, and the new lumber retaining walls would help. But these measures would not prevent even another flood like that of December 1913, which sent 6,000 cubic feet of water per second through the downtown. A greater danger was another hundred-year flood like that of 1819, which could deliver a brutal 22,000 cubic feet or more per second.[9]

The Boston engineers concluded that building a channel to carry such a flow through downtown was impractical and unnecessary. Instead, the route could be simplified by straightening the river with six cutoff channels, shortening the river by 7,050 feet—more than a mile and a half—and increasing its capacity to 12,000 cubic feet per second, half again the volume of the damaging 1913 flood. The remaining hundred-year flood volume could be held back in a retaining basin created by a dam north of Brackenridge Park near the mouth of Olmos Creek.[10]

Contrary to latter-day assumptions, Metcalf and Eddy did not recommend a cutoff for the Great Bend, either above or below ground. The

Citizens' Flood Prevention Committee provided Willard Simpson's 1911 report stating the bend could be bypassed with an underground conduit, and Metcalf and Eddy at first agreed. But the Boston engineers concluded that such a conduit would be inadequate for hundred-year floods. They were also aware of the entire project's cost, which they estimated at $4 million. City officials had made it clear that such an immediate outlay "would be impossible in the light of other urgent needs of the city," although it might be stretched over ten or twenty years.[11]

Instead of a Great Bend cutoff, the engineers recommended simply deepening the entire channel, including the Great Bend, making it a standard width of seventy feet and flanking it with steep masonry walls beside banks planted with grass. Although Metcalf and Eddy acknowledged the appeal of landscaping, they stressed that "shrubbery or trees upon the slopes must be strictly prohibited," as they "not only tend to arrest the current but also, by catching sand and gravel, to make barriers and shoals in the stream."[12]

Three months after receiving the report, city officials began its implementation. They advertised for bids to eliminate the bend above Navarro Street, enabling construction of Municipal Auditorium. They began negotiations to remove the old Guenther dam and mill near Arsenal Street, the report's first priority. Since all trees on the banks were about to be cut down to clear the channel, the Fiesta de San Jacinto Association's request to decorate trees along the river for Fiesta was denied.[13]

The sudden realization that the carefully planted cypress and other trees along the riverbanks would be removed, leaving "nothing to decorate but the walls," hit San Antonians like a bombshell.

On March 31, 1921, a wave of protest swept the city, from "men and women in all walks of life." Mayor Sam Bell and Parks Commissioner Ray Lambert were besieged with irate visitors and indignant phone calls. "It would be a disaster to take away the trees from the banks of the San Antonio River," one protester told the *Express*. "Nothing short of a

Leonard Metcalf of Boston directed a San Antonio River master flood plan in 1920.

NAVARRO ST BRIDGE 1921

By daybreak on September 10, 1921, the river had receded to its midnight level, indicated by marks on the building at left of the St. Mary's Street bridge (misidentified on the picture as Navarro Street). Debris caught in such trusses formed dams, causing water behind them to rise further.

calamity," thought another. "I think that the man who would lift an ax to remove the beautiful old trees and landmarks along the San Antonio River should be ostracized from the community," declared a third.

When Lambert was summoned to address a public meeting called on the subject at the Woman's Club the next afternoon, the mayor and the parks commissioner hastily announced that they had decided not to remove the trees after all.[14]

But the main concern of the Boston engineers had been that a flood control project start at once. "We doubt if the citizens realize the ruinous loss which would result today with the present condition of the river channels from such a flood as that of a century ago," they wrote. "When such a flood will recur, no man can say." But major flooding generally follows a hundred-year cycle. Since it had already been a hundred years since the last major flood on the San Antonio River, "a very great flood ought to be expected in the near future. . . . This disastrous flood is just as likely to occur next year as at any other time."[15]

It occurred the next year, before a full-scale flood prevention program had started.

Until nine o'clock on Friday night, September 9, 1921, the river channel was able to handle the flow from two days of heavy rains, part of an immense storm over central Texas. At Pecan Street, the river stayed within four feet of the top of the wooden embankment. But then rising waters began sweeping from Olmos Creek down the river into Brackenridge Park. More than a hundred tourist campers barely escaped with their lives as water surged two feet over the banks, pouring through the park and down nearby River Avenue/Broadway.

At 10 PM Martinez Creek went over its banks. An hour later southwestern San Antonio was under water, and Alazan Creek swept away three houses on South Laredo Street.

After 11:50 PM, for an hour and ten minutes the San Antonio River rose one foot every ten minutes. Soon after midnight it went over the top onto North St. Mary's Street. Ten minutes later it was at the base of the Navarro Street bridge near Crockett Street, and nearly half an hour after that it was in the street. When floodwaters crested at 1:45 AM Saturday, one and a half square miles of San Antonio were under water. Between two and ten feet covered three-quarters of a square mile of downtown. At Houston and North St. Mary's streets, the depth reached twelve feet.

San Antonio had seen nothing like it since 1819.

The river stayed at its crest until 3 AM. By daybreak it had receded to its midnight level. Scenes of triumph and tragedy were rife. Firemen, police, soldiers from Fort Sam Houston and civilian volunteers rescued more than 500 people. On Fourth Street, one man barely escaped from his apartment house as part of it was swept into the river. His wife and child were nowhere to be seen. Downstream an hour later, he heard cries from a house lodged against the railing of the new Navarro Street bridge. He broke through the roof and found his missing wife and child safe on a mattress floating within one foot of the ceiling.

Fort Sam Houston soldiers in a pontoon boat patrolled St. Mary's Street past the Gunter Hotel, right foreground.

The 1890 St. Mary's Street bridge survived the flood, but the scene in front of St. Mary's Catholic Church was one of desolation.

Others were not so lucky. The death toll reached fifty. One grave at San Fernando cemetery was made large enough to hold a family of six.[16]

By Saturday night downtown San Antonio resembled a war zone. Thirteen of the city's twenty-seven bridges were destroyed. Some 1,500 soldiers patrolled the watery streets. The *San Antonio Light*, its pressroom flooded, found that the press at the St. Anthony Hotel used to print menus was high and dry, and put out an edition on it.

The next day the chug of gasoline engines pumping out flooded basements mingled with the sounds of the cleanup of mud and debris. Damage estimates rose toward $10 million. Houston, Commerce and Market streets stayed closed for more than a week while more than 120 trucks—half of them from the U.S. Army—cleared debris. Resurfacing fourteen downtown streets, many paved with mesquite wood blocks which floated away, was going to take longer. The financially pressed city asked businessmen to pay a third of the cost.

During ten days of emergency food distribution, relief workers filled 6,770 grocery orders and served more than 20,600 hot meals, 57,200 sandwiches and countless cups of coffee.[17]

As relief efforts wound down, city hall had to explain how it planned to keep such a disaster from recurring. O.B. Black, the new mayor, sent engineer Clinton Kearney on a reconnaissance of Olmos Creek. A U.S. Army Corps of Engineers contingent dispatched by the War Department estimated the velocity of floodwaters at 22,000 cubic feet per second—the precise flow predicted for such a flood by Metcalf and Eddy only nine months earlier. Army engineers mapped the Olmos Creek valley and found the Boston engineers' test borings to be in an ideal location for a dam. The corps forwarded a report to Washington, but warned city officials that the army would have no part in financing a dam.[18]

Three engineers and four businesmen were named by the San Antonio Chamber of Commerce's Greater San Antonio Committee to a Flood Prevention subcommittee, which in turn formed a subcommittee of local engineers to study the matter.[19]

There were scattered complaints about building a dam or making any changes in the river, but a public meeting reflected consensus for an Olmos Creek retention dam. By the end of September local engineers were ready to start on a preliminary survey. County commissioners agreed to split the cost with the city. Citizens were warned that this was only the beginning. Reports had to be made and approved. Then a bond issue vote had to approve funding for whatever was to be done before contractors could be selected and actual work could begin.[20]

Boxes of cereal, loaves of bread and coffee cups filled relief tables during ten days of emergency food distribution after the 1921 flood.

5. Save It or Pave It?

Facing at last the full power of an unchecked river to destroy their city, San Antonians emerged from every sector to make known their hopes and fears.

Lower-income residents of western San Antonio were suspicious that problems on Alazan and San Pedro creeks would be ignored in dealing with the river in the business district. Southern San Antonians were afraid their channel would not get widened, causing floodwaters rushing through a straightened channel upstream to be dumped on the south side.

Some businessmen believed advocates of beautification were more concerned with pretty shrubs and trees than with the danger of floods and had no appreciation of the cash value of riverbed land. Women's organizations suspected those businessmen of being in cahoots with politicians to make a few dollars.

City hall wished the constant controversy would just go away, and, as costs continued to mount in those days before federal funding, worried over how it would all get paid for.

It took San Antonians nearly three years after the great flood of 1921 to reach consensus and approve $2.8 million in bonds for flood prevention. Then came the question of who would supervise the work. Boston's Metcalf and Eddy had done a thorough study, but by insisting that riverbank trees and shrubbery be removed had displeased those who worked so many years for an attractive river. Many businessmen, too, were no doubt irked at rejection of their plan for an underground conduit bypassing the Great Bend so it could be filled in for development. There was widespread sentiment against hiring any more engineers from out of town.

So it was no surprise when the Citizens' Flood Prevention Advisory Committee picked Samuel F. Crecelius, a San Antonio based engineer, to

Opposite page: Construction of the Great Bend's cutoff channel caused continuing controversy, even when completed. Efforts to make the new channel look more natural included grassy plots below, on either side of a low stream. In this 1930 view north above the Villita Street bridge, the bend's normal flow empties beside the Plaza Hotel (right) into the main channel.

plan the project. Crecelius went to work at once on the $1.5 million Olmos Dam. In two years it was finished, 80 feet high and 1,925 feet long. A roadway across the top linked the nearby San Antonio neighborhood of Laurel Heights with the five-year-old city of Alamo Heights.[1]

At dedication ceremonies on December 11, 1926, a cavalcade of automobiles led by San Antonio Mayor John W. Tobin drove onto the San Antonio side of the dam to meet cars from Alamo Heights midway. Tobin shook hands with Alamo Heights Mayor Pro Tem W.H. Hume, substituting for Mayor Robert O'Grady, who had gone deer hunting. Behind the dam stretched a newly purchased retaining basin of 1,100 acres, where a park and golf course were planned.[2]

Downstream, dangerous or flood-wrecked bridges and those where the river would be widened were being replaced. Wider streets got concrete bridges, including Jones Avenue, where the city's first iron bridge, moved from Houston Street in 1885, was dismantled. The overhead truss St. Mary's Street bridge was moved far upstream to cross the river in Brackenridge Park. At the Great Bend's historic Navarro Street/Mill Bridge crossing, a span supported by three gentle concrete arches suggested the Seine's Pont Neuf.[3]

While construction of Olmos Dam and new bridges was going on, in the fall of 1924 a crew began to clear, straighten and widen San Pedro and Alazan creeks where they joined the river south of downtown. In January 1926, a steam shovel moved into place in the channel below the mouth of San Pedro Creek near Concepción Mission. In six months a 445-foot cutoff channel eliminated a bend that meandered 2,100 feet, and the old riverbed was added to the new Concepción Park. Next to go were two smaller bends in the southern channel, one above the new park and the other near the U.S. Arsenal, where a 300-foot-wide channel cut out a 1,200-foot bend. The old Guenther Mill and its dam were removed.[4]

Two bends were removed at opposite ends of downtown. One was what remained of the Bowen's Island S-shaped bend which sent the Great

Flood Prevention Engineer Samuel Crecelius, left, goes over figures with a Corps of Engineers visitor at the Olmos Dam site.

In 1926, Olmos Dam was complete with electric lights in rectangular housings to aid nighttime drivers.

Bend west almost to the Bexar County courthouse before doubling back east and then heading south.[5] The other was the 1,830-foot double bend on the site of Municipal Auditorium, which raised the issue of river beautification with new intensity.

Property owners suggested that a fountain ten feet in diameter be in the middle of the new riverbed west of the auditorium. An operator could make spray from five concentric rings rise twenty-five feet, and six colored searchlights below the water line could evoke anything from "a waving field of ripening wheat to a crimson pyramid many feet high that looks like a huge bonfire." Mayor Tobin liked the idea so much he proposed five more fountains to be visible from key downtown intersections.

Mayor John W. Tobin was hosted by the Conservation Society on a four-boat tour of the river's natural beauty.

As the city prepared to replace strings of lights washed away by the flood and to pay for the electricity, Tobin declared: "The river is one of San Antonio's real assets, and we are to develop plans that will make it a thing of real beauty and something visitors will remember and comment on long after they leave the city."[6]

To convey the impact of the river's natural beauty, in November 1924 the young San Antonio Conservation Society treated the newly hired Samuel Crecelius, Mayor Tobin and Parks Commissioner Ray Lambert to a two-hour rowboat trip down from Ninth Street and around the Great Bend to Market Street. The ladies sought to show how preserving the river's beauty would keep a fine setting for the first Fiesta boat parade in eighteen years the next spring. They arranged for bridges over the route to be lined with cheering spectators, as in earlier river parades, but the next Fiesta parade was not held on the river.[7]

The Conservation Society established its own river-lighting committee and enlisted the input of a new honorary society member—Gutzon Borglum, new San Antonio resident and future Mount Rushmore sculptor, whose wife was a member of the Old Spanish Trail Association's river improvement committee. Borglum, who set up his studio in the abandoned 1885 Water Works pumphouse in Brackenridge Park, believed the river could be worth "millions" to the city, and urged purchase of gondolas and canoes for tourists.[8]

The first major river beautification drive since the great flood was part of a citywide cleanup for the 1928 biennial national convention of the General Federation of Women's Clubs. The five thousand members of the San Antonio Federation of Women's Club's forty-three organizations were determined to show their guests a tidy city.[9]

The Old Spanish Trail Association got the task of overseeing river cleanup. The city was persuaded to plant more flowers and shrubs along the banks and to build a flagstone riverside walk from Houston Street to Commerce Street, the route targeted by businessmen twelve years earlier. Commissioners decided to replace strings of lights with artistically placed floodlights, which one official noted would also shine on trash in the river and require it to be cleaned. Six weeks before the convention, the Texas Game, Fish and Oyster Department's director of natural resources praised San Antonio's compliance with new antipollution laws, saying that the river through San Antonio was "the cleanest in Texas." [10]

To placate both those who would deepen the Great Bend for flood control and remove its foliage and those wishing to preserve its natural beauty, flood engineer Samuel Crecelius came up with a compromise. He would build two adjacent 650-foot-long underground box culverts, but as a shortcut for flood overflow only. The river would continue as usual around the Great Bend, which would then not have to be deepened nor have its trees and shrubs stripped away. A gate at the entrance to the bend could be lowered to keep floodwaters out.[11]

Paying for the compromise was the next problem, since most of the 1924 flood prevention bond funds had been used and another $1 million had to be raised. At Mayor Tobin's insistence, Crecelius justified narrowing the culverts' total width from seventy feet to fifty, cutting right-of-way costs. If their walls were made strong enough, they could support eight-story buildings with valuable Commerce, Market and Dolorosa street frontage. Renting frontage for the buildings could bring the city a quick $200,000 to spend on flood control.[12]

But without the presence of the ailing Mayor Tobin, who was elected to a second term in absentia during an extended convalescence in San Diego, California, Crecelius ran into opposition. One faction thought a new street rather than buildings should go above the culverts. Crecelius declared that idea "definitely abandoned." He was promptly countermanded by Acting Mayor Phil Wright, who announced that the street would indeed be built.[13]

Construction had begun on the southern section of the culverts and right-of-way acquisition was proceeding on the northern part when suddenly the off-again, on-again street was off again.

Mount Rushmore sculptor Gutzon Borglum, a San Antonio resident, was an outspoken supporter of river beautification.

The dotted line marks the route of the Great Bend's cutoff channel, which eliminated the small lower bends that once extended farther east to help form Bowen's Island.

This time, businessmen rebelled against narrowing the channel to fifty feet in the first place. They petitioned to change it back to seventy feet, asserting that while water from a cloudburst north of the new dam might be held back, a cloudburst south of the dam would prove a fifty-foot channel too narrow.

But widening the channel would be "a useless waste of money," retorted Mayor Tobin, back in San Antonio. With just enough funds to finish a fifty-foot-wide channel, Tobin declared it sufficient, warning that taxpayers would not stand for another bond issue and promising, "We shall build it regardless of the protest filed."[14]

Undeterred, businessmen presented commissioners a petition with forty-five signatures requesting a seventy-foot channel as well as completion of the southern channel project to prevent "dumping floodwaters" on southside residents—including those in the fine homes along King William Street, where so many families of German origin lived that the curve in the river nearby was known as Sauerkraut Bend.[15]

By this time Mayor Tobin had died, and Crecelius was called upon to justify the fifty-foot channel. Questioned, Crecelius claimed he couldn't recollect the width of the downtown river recommended by Metcalf and Eddy—it was seventy feet, not fifty—but he cited numerous statistics, including increased costs. Commissioners went along with their engineer, and construction continued. But soon, things came unglued.[16]

The new mayor, C.M. Chambers, challenged complaining businessmen to come up with "expert advice" to support their opinion. They produced Dallas engineer O.N. Floyd. Floyd determined that the narrower conduit could carry the estimated amount of water, given its slope and assuming that debris did not block its entrance. But he found a mistake in Crecelius's calculations. Corrected, they showed the velocity of water able to enter the smaller channel would be too slow. Floyd concluded that an uncovered seventy-foot channel would be required, and that the extra cost would be less than Crecelius and the late Mayor Tobin estimated.[17]

Utility lines had to be supported, then rerouted during digging of the Great Bend's cutoff channel.

Crecelius admitted his error. Two days later, with a wider channel approved and amid reports he was being fired by the mayor, Crecelius submitted his resignation. But businessmen persuaded the mayor not to hold Crecelius responsible "for the turn things had taken." Chambers, apparently believing that Crecelius's contract was legally binding for the duration of the project, did not accept the resignation but cut the flood engineer's salary by 40 percent. Six months later the mayor closed the flood prevention office and put the program under the city engineer.[18]

This time, Crecelius resigned for good. The mayor reopened the flood prevention office and hired the Fort Worth firm of Hawley and Freese in association with O.N. Floyd. The firm hired former city engineer Hans Helland as its resident engineer.[19]

After Crecelius's departure, work on the cutoff channel remained at a near standstill for a year, while right-of-way for the wider bypass channel was acquired and another $500,000 in bonds was approved. During the lull, downtown businessmen at last saw their chance.[20]

The Great Bend's cutoff channel was now to be as wide as the Great Bend itself. Why should the expensive bypass sit empty when it could just as easily be carrying the regular flow of the Great Bend? Especially when, without drilling "scores" of artesian wells to augment the declining flow, "within ten years" the entire river would be dry anyway? The Great Bend may as well be filled in now as later.[21]

Reported one newspaper in mid-February 1928: "Prominent businessmen are said to be meeting in closed conferences, outlining a process by which they can press city commissioners to reclaim this portion of the river when the psychological time arrives—upon the completion of the 'Big Bend' cutoff." They had statistics. The Great Bend took up 294,000 square feet—nearly seven acres—of prime downtown real estate. Its value in the fast-growing city was somewhere between $2 million and $14.7 million. "At least three real estate promoters" went to work.[22]

The "promoters," however, did not get far. "Numerous civic clubs" met to oppose it. Facing a "well-defined counter-movement . . . particularly among women's clubs of the city," city officials vied with each other for the strongest condemnation of the idea.

"As long as I am in this office the Big Bend channel will never be filled up," declared Mayor Chambers. "I am absolutely against abandoning the river. In my opinion the San Antonio River is one of the biggest assets of this city." Tax Commissioner Frank Bushick "would never vote for it under any circumstances." Street Commissioner Paul Steffler believed that "to abandon the river would be a crime." He thought rerouting storm sewers which emptied into the bend would cost almost as much as the reclaimed land would be worth.[23]

The Great Bend would remain. But the businessmen had one last card to play.

One of the choicest undeveloped areas adjacent to downtown was along the southern bank of the Great Bend's southern leg—the run-down

Street Commissioner Paul Steffler was dwarfed by the depth of the cutoff channel, its starkness bringing criticism once concrete was poured.

neighborhood of La Villita, settled in Spanish times. The noose around La Villita tightened as surrounding streets were widened, improving access and opportunities. All that was missing was a direct north-south street into downtown, which filling the Great Bend would make easy.[24]

But even with the Great Bend still in place, such a street was not impossible. Neighboring businessmen quietly laid their plans.

Businessmen in the eastern part of downtown were organized as the Eastside Improvement League, headed by John H. Kirkpatrick, the "conquering hero" who had arrived on the river as Fiesta king twenty-one years before. At the close of 1928, city commissioners had promised the Improvement League that they would spend $100,000 to extend Losoya Street southeast to meet South Alamo Street at Market Street. But when funding was approved three months later, Losoya Street was instead to extend southwest, crossing Market Street to reach Villita Street.

To get there, the new forty-five-foot-wide street would pass over a parallel section of the Great Bend. At some points the entire street would overhang the river, leaving only twenty-five feet of the river's width visible from above.[25]

Eighteen days after unanimously approving the project, city commissioners swore it would never happen.

For when residents comprehended the overhang, it "met with a storm of protests from all sections of the city." Assistant City Engineer T.H. Coghill at first said his staff drew up the plans with help from the Eastside Improvement League. Then city engineers were said to have just discovered that much of the street would have to be built over the river.[26]

Armed with that revelation, Mayor Chambers branded the attempt to take space above the river "grand larceny." He made it clear that his administration would "not tolerate any such plans." The mayor refused to let a four-member delegation from the Eastside Improvement League even present arguments and termed a subsequent tour of the site, to see where the street would cross City Water Board property, a waste of time.[27]

Businessmen attemping to extend Losoya Street into La Villita in 1929 were foiled by a public outcry about its proposed overhang of the Great Bend, as shown in this drawing.

Fresh resurfacing shows on the side of the new three-story brick Police and Health Department at left, following its shortening by fifteen feet to accommodate a reconfigured cutoff channel, seen looking north from Villita Street.

The businessmen felt betrayed. A meeting with Street Commissioner Paul Steffler was marked by "heated verbal tilts." Real estate broker Ernest Altgelt complained that he had already spent $11,000 for options "on trashy shacks and dives" to line up property "under the impression that the city was ready to proceed."[28]

After the commotion died down, the Losoya Street project's $100,000 was approved as first intended, to extend the street southeast to South Alamo Street.[29] The still isolated pocket of La Villita was left to molder for another ten years until rescued in a pioneering historic preservation project. It included the outdoor Arneson River Theater, on a site that would have been in the shadow of the ill-fated bridge.

The cutoff channel project finally got moving again in March 1929, as the city also set about staking its river property line to protect against encroachments. The action was buttressed by a recent Texas Supreme Court rejection of a developer's attempt to circumvent the city and buy an abandoned river bend south of town from the state on a technicality.[30]

That favorable decision took some of the edge off the city's embarrassment as workers began tearing fifteen feet off the back of the city's new Police and Health Department Building to widen the cutoff channel. The just-completed structure was on the site of the 1855 French Building, its limestone blocks used to line the river channel from Travis Street north to the new auditorium. To the north, as concrete newly laid for the narrower channel was broken up and the channel widened, one workman died in the cave-in of an excavation beneath Commerce Street.[31]

New controversy erupted as residents saw the actual cutoff channel walls take shape. Stark concrete walls plunging to twenty-six feet straight down on either side of an empty channel did not provide the type of ambiance many San Antonians thought appropriate for their city. After one protest on the "ugliness" of the channel, Mayor Chambers grumped that it was "one of the biggest eyesores of the city and should be filled up."[32]

Then bids came in on lining the new channel south of downtown with concrete, as recommended by Hawley and Freese despite the mayor's preference for an earthen channel. Chambers, increasingly frustrated at the slow progress and at the stream of delegations which seemed to arrive laden with complaints at every step of the way, had escrow checks returned to all four bidders, fired Hawley and Freese and ordered the city engineer to build a wider channel of dirt. He said it would be more attractive than concrete and much less expensive. Declared the irascible if quotable mayor: "We are not going to line the gutters with gold."[33]

Mayor Chambers had good reason for his reluctance to spend more on flood control. Since 1924, three bond issues had provided a total of $3.9 million. But by the fall of 1929 only $150,000 was left, and two major sections were unfinished—the channel past Pioneer Flour Mills immediately south of downtown and the channel above Municipal Auditorium. As work was to start on the channel to the north, a bond issue for the $2 million that some advocated would be an even tougher sell, now that women's clubs were redescending on the beautification issue with a vengeance.[34]

Of the three bends north of downtown recommended by Metcalf and Eddy for straightening, the first, below Josephine Street, was straightened without incident early in 1929. Straightening the second and largest of the three, between Eighth and Tenth streets, began in the fall of 1928 with condemnation proceedings against recalcitrant property owners, although economic conditions would delay its completion for thirty years.[35]

But when a plan came up in 1929 to straighten the third bend, southeast of the present-day McCullough Avenue and North St. Mary's Street intersection a block past Municipal Auditorium, alarms went off.

City hall had long since dismissed Samuel Crecelius's recommendation that the entire channel from the auditorium north to Olmos Dam be straightened, widened and lined with concrete. Even Metcalf and Eddy had recommended straightening the entire channel, leaving only "substantial well-rooted trees not too close together." Now the Swiss Plaza Company proposed to loan the city $200,000 to straighten the third bend so

The upper Guenther Mill dam near Arsenal Street was dynamited to help clear the river channel south of downtown. In the background are U.S. Arsenal buildings.

Horse power still played an important part in construction in the 1920s as this cutoff channel was dug to shorten the river south of downtown San Antonio.

the company could consolidate its twelve acres for a million-dollar, twenty-four story hotel and apartment complex.[36]

The Woman's Club, the Conservation Society and a Federation of Women's Clubs committee filed formal protests with city hall. The Federation pledged "united opposition" to any measure to further change the course of the river upstream or remove any vegetation at all, and later went so far as to declare that the river was "being constantly menaced by the selfishness and greed of promoters and politicians." When Swiss

Plaza agreed to both donate the land and pay for the cutoff in exchange for the old riverbed, city commissioners accepted, although the deal went no further due to the worsening Depression.[37]

To mute Federation of Women's Clubs fears that river water would be permanently diverted into the Great Bend's cutoff channel, and to soften the starkness of the dry cutoff channel's high concrete walls, the city planted grass, flowers and low shrubs on sod laid within the channel on either side of an open sixteen-foot median strip, which carried a small flow of water piped in to give the appearance of a natural stream.[38]

After a drought in the summer of 1927 threatened to dry up the river, there was no debate over installing a pump—an electric one, this time—at a well near the headwaters to put water back in. The next summer an underground sprinkler system was installed to keep the river's downtown banks green. A visiting official of the Southern States Art League told local artists that the river was "the most beautiful thing you have; it has anything New York has got beaten a thousand blocks."[39]

By the time most elements of its flood prevention project were complete, the City of San Antonio in 1929 at last hired a professional city planner. Public debate could now shift entirely from "Where should the river go?" back to, simply, "How should it look?"

Margaret Goodspeed holds a one-and-a-half pound crawfish caught in the river south of downtown in 1927.

With the Great Bend protected from flooding, an imaginative plan for its development entitled "Shops of Aragon and Romula" was first presented by Robert H.H. Hugman in 1929.

6. The Beautification Debate

As businessmen in 1928 pursued their main chance to get the Great Bend drained and filled, a young architect named Robert Harvey Harold Hugman was back in San Antonio. Fresh from New Orleans, where efforts to preserve the historic French Quarter were under way, he could see that his home town also had a distinctive river ambiance to save. In the enthusiasm of his twenties, he came up with a plan on how to do it.

In pursuit of his vision Hugman would be accepted by the city, then rejected, accepted and finally rejected again, leaving him, in 1940, embittered on the subject for most of his remaining forty years. But he lived to see San Antonio enjoy the rich fruits of his tenacity, and to receive some of the recognition that was his due.[1]

Robert Hugman was an anomaly among the prominent architects building San Antonio in the early decades of the century. Many—Alfred Giles, James Riely Gordon, George Willis, pioneer river designer Harvey Page—came from somewhere else, drawn by the new construction in one of the nation's fast-growing cities. Many leading architects who did grow up in San Antonio—Ralph Cameron, Atlee B. and Robert M. Ayres—had sterling credentials from the northeast and often from Europe and enjoyed close ties to the local business and social establishment.

But Hugman, born to a working class family on San Antonio's near south side, graduated from Brackenridge High School and went on to study architecture and design less than a hundred miles from San Antonio, at the University of Texas in Austin. Hugman's perspective came not from the first hand observations others could bring from the Old World, but from books.[2]

"We read descriptions of the old cities of Spain," Hugman wrote, "of a narrow, winding street barred to vehicular traffic yet holding the best

Robert Hugman made his River
Walk proposal at the age
of twenty-seven.

shops, clubs, banks and cafes; prosperous, yet alluring, with its sha-
dowed doorways and quaint atmosphere. . . . It occurred to me that such
a street in the very heart of our growing city would do much to enhance
its interest and naught to impair its progress."[3]

Hugman envisioned beginning such a street where river planners had
been focusing their thoughts for the previous sixteen years: near the cen-
trally-located Houston Street bridge. The entrance was apparently to be a
new passage cut through the three-story red brick Book Building at the
southwest corner of the bridge. To the rear, a "typical old Spanish patio"
would provide a view of the river from above.

Visitors would descend along a narrow cobblestone street, with the
shops of "Aragon" built of old stone and brick on either side. The river
would come into view again at the foot of the street, near the start of the
new cutoff channel, where the original channel turned 90 degrees into the
Great Bend and where an outdoor cafe would be located.

From the cafe, a footbridge would arch the start of the cutoff channel
to the southern bank of the Great Bend and the shops of "Romula," a
name Hugman invented. Flagstone walks would meander past river-level
shops and restaurants, similar to those of Aragon and protected from
flooding by the cutoff channel's floodgates. After the bend turned sharply
south and then west, the channel would divide into two streams through
"a sunken garden of loveliness to compare with the famous Gardens of
the Alcazar or the Alhambra." Spanish-style gondolas would ferry visitors along the river to the Plaza Hotel at the end of the Great Bend.[4]

Robert Hugman took his plan to a leading advocate of the river's preservation, Amanda (Mrs. Lane) Taylor, then chairman of the San Antonio
Conservation Society's river committee. Armed with her encouragement,
Hugman in 1929 carried his plan to city hall, where he found a ready, if
short-term, ally—the mayor himself.[5]

Hugman's plan was heartily endorsed by Mayor C.M. Chambers as a
concept "that will do much to preserve and enhance the distinctiveness of

Hugman urged riverside commercial development, as in this sketch of the west bank north of Commerce Street, where restaurants were later built.

San Antonio." Moreover, the mayor was "reasonably sure" that commissioners would adopt it.

With that, Hugman the next month presented his plan at a meeting of thirty business, civic and political leaders, including the mayor and two commissioners. He stressed that his plan was of great commercial value and must not be separated into parts but, "like a stage setting designed and directed by one mind to produce the proper unity of thought and feeling," needed to be carried out as a unit, "shops, lighting effects, advertising—everything." Most of those present pledged support. Two days later, the text of Hugman's proposal was published in the *Light*.[6]

In scarcely two weeks, however, Hugman's plan was sidelined not by opponents of river beautification, but by those dedicated to a long-sought goal of progressive San Antonians—a comprehensive city plan.

Hiring a professional planner had been a prime objective of the civic reformers who captured control of city hall in 1912. Led by Rena Maverick (Mrs. Robert B.) Green, the cause was taken up thirteen years later by the new Conservation Society. With renewed public support and with businessmen increasingly frustrated over the tangle of rampant growth,

National city planner
Harland Bartholomew
recommended a strictly
natural river setting.

Mayor Chambers at the end of 1928 began appointing fifty-six San Antonians to an advisory City Plan Committee.[7]

Within six months the committee wanted to hire Harland Bartholomew and Associates, a leading city planning firm based in St. Louis, to undertake a project costing $40,000. Mayor Chambers, in the midst of a fiscal economy drive, thought that far too much to spend. With a decision imminent, the mayor brought up Hugman's counter-proposal: use Hugman's plan for the river and get a master plan for the city through a nationwide competition offering $7,000 in prizes, a significant savings.[8]

Leaders of the City Plan Committee, their hard-sought goal threatened at the last minute, took direct aim at Robert Hugman.

Hugman's plan was no more than an "idle dream," charged City Plan Committee Chairman Newton H. White, a Realtor who headed the Chamber of Commerce. His committee had already studied the river, White told commissioners, and to adopt Hugman's plan would set his group's work back six months. In any event, he added, Harland Bartholomew himself recognized the need to preserve San Antonio's individuality and the river, and local city plan competitions had failed to produce results.[9]

After three forceful speakers followed White, commissioners postponed a decision for three days. Then White and three of the twenty Plan Committee members present pleaded the case for Bartholomew. When two others asked commissioners to make do instead with local architects and engineers and suggested two possible candidates, the two mentioned rose and opposed the suggestion that they be hired. City commissioners agreed with the City Plan Committee and hired Harland Bartholomew.[10]

Robert Hugman was assigned to political limbo, his supporters in the Conservation Society immobilized by their desire to see a city plan undertaken by a planner of Bartholomew's stature. That fall, the City Federation of Women's Clubs sent a resolution to city commissioners asking that Hugman at least be hired as the river's landscape architect. But the mayor said the question of Hugman's employment would have to wait. In the meantime, work on a city plan could finally begin.[11]

The City Plan Committee's choice of a planner was a good one. Harland Bartholomew, 40, had been director of planning for the city of St. Louis since 1916 and was doing extensive consulting work. His firm's policy was to work closely with municipal governments, building consensus for the work ahead. As a measure of its success, during the first six years of the 1920s the firm did twenty of the nation's eighty-seven comprehensive city plans, nearly twice as many as its closest competitor.[12]

Harland Bartholomew took an active personal role in the San Antonio project. He gave particular attention to river improvements, a subject dominating his first official visit late in 1929. In three years, the Depression notwithstanding, his firm produced a 400-page comprehensive city plan. It covered streets, transportation, transit, zoning, recreation and civic art, a category with a section titled "Proposed Treatment of the San Antonio River in the Central Business District."[13]

The planner found the San Antonio River "one of the most distinctive and commendable features in the character of San Antonio. . . . To the visitor this is a picture not easily forgotten." He suggested a parkway along the river from downtown north through Brackenridge Park to help make up for the city's deficiency in parkways and boulevards. But the most detailed river analysis was reserved for downtown.

Bartholomew's solution for the Great Bend was markedly different from Hugman's. He recommended that river-oriented commercial activity be kept at street level, along a mall covering the unsightly cutoff channel. Landscaping would return the river below to a natural state, making it a contemplative linear park through the heart of the busy city.[14]

To restore the river's role as a scenic asset, Bartholomew prescribed groupings of water elm, sycamore, cypress and pecan trees to provide shade, screen backs of buildings and overhang the water. Vines would climb walls and lattices and provide ground cover, while native flowering shrubs broke up retaining walls' straight lines and produced masses of color. Low flowers and reeds would line the channel. Beside bridges, tall

Instead of adding commercial intrusions as Robert Hugman urged, in 1933 the City Plan Committee endorsed the Bartholomew plan of doing only more plantings along the Great Bend, shown in 1930 by the new Smith-Young Tower.

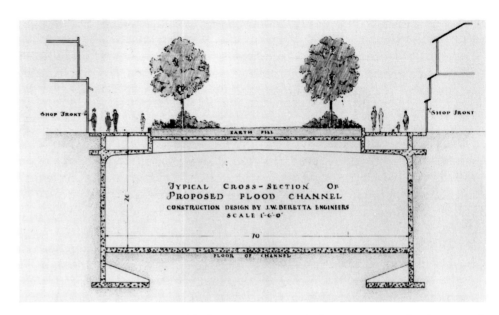

Unlike Hugman's plan to cut doorways in the backs of buildings at river level for Spanish-style shops, Bartholomew's plan would put a concrete cover over the unsightly cutoff channel for a Spanish-style pedestrian mall and cut doors in the backs of buildings at street level for shops.

evergreen cypresses would frame views of the river, with date and banana palms adding a tropical note. Only a few benches were suggested, and general recreation was ruled out as too distracting. Outside the Great Bend, where such landscaping would slow floodwaters, would be only groups of low shrubs and flowers and vines on masonry walls.[15]

Bartholomew's proposal included river-oriented Spanish-style shops and restaurants, as Hugman wanted, but these were not to disrupt the pastoral nature of the riverbanks. Rather they would be kept at street level, lining both sides of a unique pedestrian mall created over a reinforced concrete covering of the roundly condemned "ugly and glaring" cutoff channel. According to Bartholomew, engineers believed a covered cutoff could still handle a hundred-year flood.

The new mall over the covering would feature ten-foot walkways on either side of a fifty-foot-wide grassy median, landscaped with cacti and native plants able to thrive on two feet of earth fill. At each end a fountain and an overlook would offer vistas of the main river channel. Backs of buildings which ended at the sheer channel walls would be instead at the edge of the new mall. Doorways cut in the backs of existing buildings and colorful shops built on vacant lots would provide 950 feet of retail frontage, generating tax revenues to pay for the project.[16]

Neatly though this solution may have addressed beautification of both the river and the yawning cutoff channel, by the time the plan was finished and formally recommended to city commissioners it was March 1933. The full force of the Depression had plunged downtown San Antonio into a slump from which it would not recover for nearly four decades. The building boom had come to an abrupt end, city hall lost nearly 20 percent of a year's municipal operating funds in the city's worst bank failure and there were massive layoffs of city workers.[17]

In another break in continuity at city hall, in the month the plan was presented C.M. Chambers became San Antonio's fourth mayor in twenty-one years to die while in office. Some of the recommendations, including the city's first zoning and a street plan, had been implemented along the way, but major recommendations would obviously go on hold.[18]

Despite the lack of action on either Hugman's or Bartholomew's plans, the city did not abandon river beautification. Renewed efforts focused on the block between the northern St. Mary's and Navarro street bridges, where the narrow bank below Crockett Street was known at the turn of the century as Tobin Terrace. In 1934 the City Parks Department under Commissioner Jacob Rubiola restored a riverside cascade built ten years earlier behind St. Mary's College. The next spring, parks workers enhanced the 1913 river project by building ten riverbank flowerbeds of native stone on both sides of the same block. Meanwhile, relief workers lined 3,000 feet of the river in Brackenridge Park with rock walls.[19]

Then the Texas Centennial lent the spark to revive Hugman's plans.

In 1935, the Alamo Chapter of the Daughters of the American Revolution made "beautifying and conserving the natural charm of the

With no action on either the Hugman or Bartholomew plans, in 1935 the city enhanced its earlier river project by adding flowerbeds.

To the strains of mariachi music, local Daughters of the American Revolution, who made river beautification a project for 1936, christen a new boat for river rides.

San Antonio River" one of its centennial projects and enlisted the backing of Parks Commissioner Rubiola. Soon the DAR heard a presentation from Robert Hugman, by then a consulting landcape architect for the Works Progress Administration, who was still promoting his plan to all who would listen. Unable to get the city to pay for lighting the river at night between Travis and Nueva streets, the ladies got the money from the city's Centennial Association. At the opening of Fiesta week in the centennial year of 1936, they christened two motorboats beginning commercial trips from the Houston Street bridge.[20]

Next came Venetian Night and the first Fiesta week boat parade in twenty-nine years, sponsored by Plaza Hotel Manager Jack White and Mexican Business Men's Association President Andrew Morales, who got plans for the boats' decorations in Mexico City. More than 10,000 people crowded riverbanks east of the Plaza Hotel to watch a parade of eighteen decorated boats. Two bands played, a company of dancers performed and flower girls in Mexican costumes strolled the banks.[21]

The next day, gondola rides began at a landing near White's prestigious twelve-story Plaza Hotel, built at the corner where the bedraggled end of the Great Bend met the cutoff channel—which passed its first big test in mid-1935, when heavy rains left twenty feet of water behind Olmos Dam and floodwaters were carried safely through downtown.[22]

The outpouring for Venetian Night showed White that San Antonians had not lost their enthusiasm for the river. And as a businessman, he saw more appeal in Hugman's commercially oriented river plan than in Bartholomew's strictly pastoral proposal. Plus there was an opportunity to give the Plaza an environment more commensurate with its status.

White organized riverside property owners into the San Antonio River Beautification Committee. The group hired Robert Hugman and got WPA District Engineer Edwin P. Arneson to make surveys and drawings of a project to submit for WPA funding. After three months of study, by Fiesta in 1938 the drawings were on display at the Plaza Hotel. They showed terraced banks with walkways and a theater on one side of the river screened from seats on the other by a curtain of sprayed water. Buildings' rear entrances were "changed into beautiful front entrances of shops, cafes, etc., so that visitors and residents of the city could shop from a gondola."[23]

"Other cities can have beautiful parks, great zoos, magnificent stadiums and other attractions," said White, echoing earlier generations of San Antonio River planners. "But we know of no city that has a beauty spot such as we propose to make of the river. . . . It would attract unlimited publicity to the city. . . . A boat ride on the San Antonio River would attract tourists to this city as the gondolas do to Venice."[24]

The committee came up with a nearly $400,000 project to beautify a mile and quarter of the river south from Municipal Auditorium to the end of the Great Bend—which was by then called the Big Bend, since elimination of other bends had reduced the scale of comparison. White and Judge Claude V. Birkhead, with advertising man Tom McNamara, asked the city for $50,000. The committee would collect $40,000 from property owners along the river to qualify for WPA funds for the remainder. But commissioners said the city couldn't come up with the money.[25]

Money could be raised, commissioners pointed out, if an Improvement District were organized and voted to tax itself for $75,000 in bonds to qualify. But only four owners of real property lived within the proposed district's boundaries, and two were against it. White found a loophole: voting residents could be owners of just personal property, even nothing more than a wrist watch. That qualified 103 residents of White's Plaza Hotel. Of the 76 votes cast, 74 were in favor and 2 were opposed.[26]

By the end of 1938, most of the remaining WPA funds were in place, thanks to the support of state WPA Director Henry P. Drought, a San Antonian, and to the lobbying of San Antonio Congressman Maury Maverick, who pleaded the case with his friend Franklin D. Roosevelt. "Harold," the President instructed Secretary of the Interior Harold Ickes, "give Maury the money for his rivah so he will stop bothering me."[27]

Robert Hugman's river plan was revived following the success in 1936 of Venetian Night and the first boat parade in twenty-nine years.

7. Transforming the Great Bend

On the morning of March 29, 1939, a WPA band played as three hundred San Antonians gathered at the Market Street bridge to watch Jack White break ground for the San Antonio River Walk with a golden shovel. Those present knew the moment was auspicious, but could not know how pivotal it would become for their beloved river and city, even for other cities far away.

For fifty years San Antonians had sought to recapture their river's charm, which so enchanted the earliest citizens and their visitors. A long succession of committees, leagues and federations advanced the cause, bending engineering decisions toward their vaguely defined goal.

Now the decades of discussions and debates culminated with the start of a carefully considered transformation of the Great Bend into a creation that would itself evolve—haltingly, during the course of the next half century—into a model for river development in cities throughout the world.

Following the groundbreaking, work began on a careful mix of commercial and park development to romantically evoke San Antonio's Spanish origins. Robert Hugman was the architect and Walter H. Lilly the chief engineer. Setting aside plans for Aragon's cobblestone lane from Houston Street down to the river, they focused on creating a semitropical setting of water and exotic landscaping for the shops of Romula.[1]

After that, beside Romula's adobe shops Hugman foresaw a potter at his wheel, a basket weaver, flower sellers, visitors in Spanish-style gondolas poled past floating islands while swans and water pheasants bobbed in the water. "The river tempo, slow and lazy" would contrast

Opposite page: With the Great Bend's flow diverted through the cutoff channel, workmen prepare to build the Arneson River Theater's stage house as the entry gate goes up at top right. At upper left is the 511 Villita St. house later restored by the Conservation Society.

Varied sidewalk designs add a sense of anticipation and discovery on the River Walk.

with the bustle at street level above. Understated design was of paramount importance. Said Hugman: "I'll die if it looks like Hollywood."[2]

But first, practical engineering matters had to be tended to. River-level shops must not be at risk during high waters. At the beginning of the bend a gate was designed with Spanish-style arches through which steel gates could drop to prevent flooding.

Then came the problem of the fall of the river, which descended seven feet through the Great Bend. At the downstream end by the Plaza Hotel, a new dam six feet high brought the bend's water level to a near-uniform depth, leaving a one-foot drop to maintain a gentle flow. Project Engineer Robert H. Turk, while also directing more river channeling in Brackenridge Park, supervised building the dam in a wide arc for a picturesque waterfall into the downstream channel. Shallow places in the drained riverbed had to be dug out and deep ones filled to gain a consistent depth of some three and a half feet, deep enough for gondoliers' poles but shallow enough to guard against drowning for anyone falling from a gondola or from sidewalks near the river's edge.[3]

While the bend was drained, existing plants and shrubs were temporarily transplanted elsewhere. Trees were kept watered with their roots protected. Decayed limbs were pruned, hollow trunks plugged with concrete and weak trees braced. Plans were made to plant 11,734 more trees and shrubs, 1,500 banana trees and 1,489 square yards of grass.[4]

Hugman wrote that George Surkey's 1913 river walls, extending starkly above the water line, "confined the water to an extremely unnatural bank line, but practically all of the new walls will be concealed and the result will be much more pleasing." The texture of sidewalks, in intervals of cobblestone, pea gravel and flagstone, would aid a sense of discovery at every turn. Pebbled concrete panels featured nearly a dozen designs, some with colored effects. Hugman had their walkability tested by women wearing shoes with different types of heels.[5]

Where the North Presa Street bridge left no space for a path beneath, Hugman had supports built for a walkway appearing to float on the water. He relandscaped the cascade behind the old St. Mary's College—later the hotel La Mansion del Rio—and built around it a crescent-shaped flagstone walkway, with water flowing between the stones from condensation piped from the nearby Majestic Theater's air conditioning system.[6]

New stairways from bridges down to the River Walk were self-supporting and unattached to the bridges, preventing separation due to vibration at street level and movement of water-soaked earth below. On some a rustic note was added by steps and railings of cedar logs, later replaced with more durable stone steps and metal railings. Elaborate iron gates were designed for street-level entrances.[7]

For San Antonio to become the "Venice of America," pedestrian bridges had to be high enough for gondoliers to remain standing as they passed beneath. Two new sharply arching bridges of native limestone provided one of the River Walk's signature features.

The largest new feature was an open-air theater on the final leg of the Great Bend. Its stage, tile-roofed dressing rooms and backdrop of three stone arches were built on the north bank, below the San Antonio Water Works/City Water Board pumping station. A bridge arching from stage right reached the gently curving, sharply rising south bank, where new concrete bleachers were pounded to make them appear carved from natural rock. Seats could be entered at river level or from above, through the concurrent La Villita project—also championed by Maury Maverick, the former congressman and newly elected mayor.

The complex was to be called the Broadcast Theater, where radio performances of miracle plays of the Spanish Southwest and "other native drama" could originate. It was renamed in memory of Edwin Arneson, the helpful WPA engineer who died before the project began.[8]

Work started with great enthusiasm. Hugman noticed that as he and Robert Turk discussed the project on site, "all the workmen within ear-

Robert Hugman, bending on stairs at right, gives advice prior to cutting of the bridge rail to open access to Crockett Street. The rustic cedar steps were later replaced with stone.

Raw concrete and stone in unfamiliar shapes plus the desolate appearance of the drained Great Bend brought increasing opposition to Hugman's work. The building at right is now the hotel La Mansion del Rio.

shot would stop and listen intently to our conversation. We then purposely talked loud enough for them to hear and understand. They would then return to their work with added vigor and purpose."[9]

But the light color of unseasoned limestone blocks in unfamiliar shapes of bridges and theaters, and the unconventional designs of sidewalks and other features, stood in sharp contrast to the previous pastoral nature of the Great Bend. The drained channel, in muddy disarray with its banks barren in the temporary absence of former plantings, made the disparity appear even more jarring. Only three months into the project Hugman was having to explain that his Spanish-Mexican design would soon be in "as naturalistic setting as possible," emphasizing, "Everything is being done to avoid a raw, new, garish effect."[10]

Two days before Christmas in 1939, Jack White ceremoniously turned the valve to close the cutoff channel gates, diverting water back into the Great Bend for the first time since March. Planting could then begin. Work on the final phase, lining the channel from the start of the Great Bend north to Municipal Auditorium, would start in the new year.[11]

Yet concern over the Great Bend's appearance continued. It extended even to the Conservation Society, worrying both cofounders—Emily Edwards, one of Hugman's teachers at Brackenridge High School, who met with Hugman on the subject, and parks activist Rena Maverick Green, a good friend of Hugman's mother and a member of the former City Plan Committee which endorsed the Bartholomew plan for a purely natural river setting. In January 1940 the society passed a resolution protesting the project's "desecration of the beauties of San Antonio." At the urging of one member—the wife of Jack White—a critique on the "excessive stone work" was sent to Hugman. Resolved a group of artists headed by Mrs. Green: "We think that the stone work is much over-done."[12]

Hugman replied that the softening effect of subsequent plantings would take care of the objections, although he acknowledged that "this is hard to visualize at the present time."[13]

To take the River Walk beneath the sharply angled North Presa Street bridge embankment, Hugman designed a walkway to appear, once the Bend was refilled, to be floating on the water.

Such visualization, however, was beyond the capacity of even the eminent architect Atlee B. Ayres, who as chairman of a committee more than a quarter century earlier backed a more conservative river project. Ayres thought Hugman's work "was not done in a simple manner," declaring flatly, "With few exceptions, it is a most unwise expenditure and will be a source of ridicule to our tourist friends and others. I do hope that we won't have any more of this mis-named river beautification."[14]

Hugman found it difficult to compromise with his critics. When the city recommended he hire a particular landscape architect, he refused on the grounds that it would be a political hiring at too high a salary.[15]

Since Hugman would not shift his emphasis to landscaping on his own, Mayor Maury Maverick, who was catching much of the criticism, decided to force him to by simply cutting Hugman's supply of the offending material. Agreeing with a critic that too much stone may have

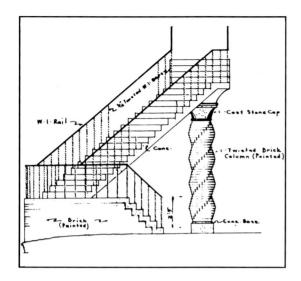

Hugman's stairway from Crockett Street.

been used, Mayor Maverick replied, "In line with your ideas I have eliminated a large amount that they originally planned to use."[16]

When Hugman found his materials going instead to another federally funded project—La Villita—he was furious. He collected copies of vouchers for the diverted materials and presented them to Judge Claude Birkhead, one of his original backers, who sat on the river project board. But the board, chaired by Jack White, who had already fallen out with Hugman, in March 1940 unanimously fired him.[17]

Hugman did not publicly admit his whistle-blowing ploy for another thirty years. He charged instead that he was the victim of "machine politics" for not hiring the landscape architect urged on him by city hall, and threatened legal action against the city.[18]

Robert Hugman had supervised the project for slightly less than one year. Though only half done, most of its now familiar stonework—walks, bridges, stairways, the Arneson River Theater—was in place. Hugman, never a member of the local architect establishment, ended his career as an architect employed at Randolph Air Force Base, still seeing himself as an outsider. "You know," he ruefully said later of his dismissal, "a poor boy does not fight city hall."[19]

For his part, Mayor Maverick explained to the press merely that "work on the project has reached a point where less formal rock architecture and more landscaping with shrubs, trees and flowers is needed." To continue the project the mayor endorsed Jack White's recommendation of the young architect J. Fred Buenz, a member of the city's park advisory and planning board.[20] Reassured, the Conservation Society in the fall of 1940 moved its fall festival from San José Mission to the banks of the river as a River Jubilee, featuring a parade of boats.[21]

On March 13, 1941, the Works Progress Administration formally turned over the completed River Walk to the City of San Antonio. The 21-block project included 8,500 feet of riverbank downtown as well as in Brackenridge Park, with a total of 17,000 feet of new sidewalks, 11,000 cubic yards of masonry, 31 stairways and 3 dams and some 4,000 trees, shrubs and plants, plus benches of stone, cement and cedar. Wrote Mayor Maverick in his final report: "We believe that in all the United States there is no city in which a river has been made a more attractive resort for all people."[22]

An estimated 50,000 people lined the River Walk on April 21, disregarding a light evening rain to dedicate the project and watch the first of what finally became an annual Fiesta parade of boats. The Fiesta king, by then designated "Antonio," was chosen from members of the Texas Cavaliers, who would sponsor the parades. In 1941, King Antonio XXIII was, conveniently, George Friederich, whose Friederich Company shops could make the king's galvanized iron barge. He commanded a flotilla of fifty plywood-bottomed boats, built on the two lowest floors of the Smith-Young Tower beside the river and festooned with flowers.[23]

The procession, with King Antonio's float at the end, left the Ursuline Academy landing below Municipal Auditorium about 8 PM and lasted for an hour and a quarter. Beneath the Crockett Street bridge the flotilla passed the reviewing stand, where Mayor Maverick announced descriptions of each craft.

The parade was led by a police canoe followed by a group of masked operators of foot-powered paddle boats, purchased from San Francisco's international exposition two years earlier. On the bow of the float of the Third U.S. Army commander, Maj. Gen. H.J. Brees, was the American flag in flowers, and on its stern was the flowered national emblem. Sides of one boat were covered with balloons, occupants of another waved lighted sparklers, and in a third "hula" girls moved only their hands and arms to avoid rocking their boat. At the Arneson River Theater participants disembarked for a reception in the newly-restored La Villita above.[24]

The drizzle continued through the evening. The mayor wore a raincoat and there seemed to be plenty of umbrellas. But trouble was ahead for utility company manager Victor Braunig's float. The boat was decorated,

At the Fiesta boat parade dedicating the River Walk in 1941, King Antonio XXIII—George Friederich—addresses the crowd while Mayor Maury Maverick, left, and Jack White, in the uniform of the Texas Cavaliers, look on.

The newly completed Spanish-style structure at the start of the Great Bend enclosed gates to divert all river water into the cutoff channel in case of flooding.

appropriately, with strings of electric lights powered by a small generator rigged on board. But rain seeped into the light sockets, short-circuiting the system and knocking out the generator. In the confusion the system's operator fell overboard, and the boat was left to continue darkened for the rest of the trip.[25]

So did San Antonio's River Walk project end its formative phase, buffeted by unexpected events and also left at the end of its course with an appearance changed from what was planned. Robert Hugman was no longer on board, his guiding inspiration short-circuited by disagreements with his original supporters. Soon the energies of Maury Maverick, defeated for re-election in 1941, were also gone, as he and the rest of the nation coped with World War II, which ended thoughts of additional work on the River Walk and countless other projects.

The result was not all that Robert Hugman had wished for more than a decade earlier. The Shops of Aragon and Romula had not been built. "Aragon," the cobblestone entry lane descending from Houston Street to the river, did not even exist. Nor were there yet adobe or any other shops in "Romula," along the bend itself. There would be no "sunken garden of loveliness," no curtain of water to screen the river theater stage, no decorative street-level gates, no potters at their wheels nor swans nor water pheasants floating on the lazy stream. San Antonio would not become, as *The New York Times* reported the plans intended, "the city where you shop from gondolas."[26]

Yet the single-minded architect Robert Harvey Harold Hugman had accomplished what none of the well-connected architects or nationally known planners or politicians or prosperous businessmen had been able to achieve for decades. The Great Bend of the San Antonio River was now transformed with a uniform design executed with uncommon flair, one which, given the unique conditions of that stretch of the river, could be reproduced in few other places, if anywhere.

When critics and depressed economies and wars had had their day, Robert Hugman's San Antonio River Walk would be there to welcome the world.

Original benches designed by Robert Hugman continue to add a rustic note to the River Walk.

8. From Hugman to HemisFair

Created as war clouds gathered over Europe, the two-year-old San Antonio River Walk found itself playing a bit part on the home front in the waging of World War II.

In the spring of 1943, with Secretary of the Treasury Henry Morgenthau Jr. in town to help kick off a national $13 billion war bonds drive, the River Walk was picked to publicize local war bonds sales, part of the "greatest publicity and advertising campaign" in the nation's history. Crowds gathered along the River Walk below the Houston Street bridge to watch workers representing five divisions of the war bond "army" race in amphibious jeeps piloted on the river by U.S. Army drivers.[1]

The newly-completed river project was kept in the public consciousness during of the war years by Fiesta boat parades and the Conservation Society's fall festival and jubilee along the River Walk. Soldiers were welcomed home with their own boat parade in July of 1945.[2]

After the end of World War II, however, San Antonio's River Walk got lost in the changes sweeping the city. Lacking the commercial half of Robert Hugman's master plan for both natural and commercial development, the River Walk was generally neglected by the public and its ambiance was scorned by businessmen, who violated one of its most pastoral settings by building a bridge across the river for a parking garage. In 1941 Hugman held to his cause by becoming the first to open a river-level office, but no one followed suit. After the war the River Walk became a haven for vagrants and was declared off-limits for military personnel.[3]

Yet the post-war years proved to be the incubation period for the River Walk's phenomenal future success. Its seeds would sprout quietly and bear fruit as suddenly as did those sown before the civic reform movement of 1912, and with results even more dramatic.

Opposite page: In 1946, Casa Rio, below the Commerce Street bridge, became the first business to open on the River Walk. In the 1950s it also offered cruises in covered gondolas.

In 1943, the two-year-old River Walk was the setting for a race of amphibious jeeps to promote a national war bonds drive.

In October 1946, Alfred Beyer opened the Casa Rio Mexican Restaurant in the excavated basement of his street-level appliance store beside the Commerce Street bridge. He built stairs down to the river, preserved the indoor remnants of a Spanish-era riverside home revealed during the work and painted the name on the upper side of the building so it would be visible at street level. The first business at the river level, it was inspired less by devotion to the river than by economic necessity. "His appliance sales were being taken away by the department stores," said Beyer's grandson Bill Lyons. "He had to do something."[4]

In another significant event that fall, a two-month drought ended with a rainfall of more intensity than that which had caused the great flood twenty-five years earlier. Property damage exceeded $2.6 million, and four lives were lost. Thanks to Olmos Dam, most destruction was in watersheds of the San Antonio River's other tributaries. The river downtown was deep but did not overflow its banks. With the cutoff gates closed, there was little damage around the Great Bend.[5]

After the flood of 1946, the U.S. Army Corps of Engineers spent five years studying and designing an expanded flood control plan for the San Antonio River. It was funded not by the frequent, hotly-debated municipal bond issues that had to finance the pioneering work of the 1920s, but by a newly authorized Bexar County flood control tax.

The work was supervised by the young San Antonio River Authority. Among improvements along thirty-one miles of the river, the convoluted bends at Ninth Street and at McCullough Avenue were at last straightened, as was one to the south near Roosevelt Avenue. Flood control on the River Walk was fine-tuned with construction of a tainter gate midway through the cutoff channel and a gate to replace the dam at the upper end of the Great Bend.[6]

Also, Mayor Chambers's earthen channel through the King William Street neighborhood's Sauerkraut Bend south of downtown was straightened further and finally lined with concrete, and later landscaped to great effect. The Corps of Engineers was persuaded to adjust the new channel to preserve a row of giant cypress trees. But in southern Bexar County, the newly straightened, widened and deepened channel diverted water from the historic San Juan Acequia. It took litigation led by the Conservation Society to get the new channel dam modified so the acequia could again bring water to adjacent fields.[7]

Meanwhile, the River Walk, sheltered from colder weather above, was turned into a virtual subtropical botanical garden under Stewart King, the city forester. Its lone annual event, the Cavaliers' Fiesta river parade, was joined in 1947 by the River Art Group's winter River Art Show. Ten years later, as security improved with park rangers' regular patrols, the Alamo Kiwanis Club began its summertime Fiesta Noche del Rio in the river theater. Still, the only river-level businesses were Casa Rio and the Chinese restaurant Lung Jeu, below the Commerce Street bridge.[8]

One of Robert Hugman's worst fears seemed about to be realized when the city finally sought to energize the River Walk by turning to Hollywood.

In 1960, business leaders led by appliance wholesaler David Straus persuaded the City of San Antonio and the Chamber of Commerce to finance a River Walk study by California's Marco Engineering Company, designers of Disneyland. Firm members easily found the River Walk "run down and in need of repainting, improved lighting, better housekeeping, police protection and additional park benches." Their solution was "intensive application of creative design to the selection and arrangement of props and dressings."[9] Translation: Add glitter.

Two pedestrian pontoon bridges were to be built and opened for barges vending souvenirs and food. A water tank near the Arneson River Theater was to be encased in simulated stone for "an authentic ancient appearance." Mexican colonial-style stores and restaurants would be surrounded by "considerable show and entertainment." To get "maximum patronage," one to three fiestas were to be held each month, creating a "River of Fiestas" along a River Walk which, Marco recommended, within

Not just a ticker tape parade through the streets but a boat parade along the River Walk welcomed San Antonio soldiers home from World War II in 1945.

In the 1940s and 50s the picturesque River Walk was mostly deserted. Here a canoe and a hand-poled barge carrying spectators in canvas chairs enter the Arneson River Theater.

three years should be extended far upstream to Brackenridge Park. All this was to draw 700,000 persons in the first year alone.[10]

Like a target suddenly thrown into the air, the very idea of a Disney-land designer planning to exploit the hallowed—if neglected—River Walk startled many San Antonians and galvanized them to take aim on exactly how the river's development should be properly continued. Its glitz doomed the Marco study, but it precipitated a critical turning point in the evolution of the San Antonio River Walk. One response came from San Antonian O'Neil Ford, considered by many to be the state's leading architect. He summed up the basis for Hugman's planning for the Great Bend, which remained the basic philosophy for River Walk development.

"For many years," wrote Ford, "many of us who love the peaceful river and its green embankments have talked and studied this matter of making the river even more lovely by the installation of shops, restaurants, etc. along its course. But never have we thought that such development should be allowed to cover one square foot of the river development proper. Rather, we have conceived of such development on the adjoining private property, some rotting buildings being replaced entirely and some shops being tucked under the river side of sound existing buildings. . . . We must somehow leave our most beautiful public areas to the public use, and enhance them by private development alongside."[11]

For fifty years city officials had wrestled over whether local or out-of-town experts should plan the future of San Antonio's river. In 1913 city hall did not hire Kansas City's George Kessler but completed a major beautification project directed by its own river commissioner, George Surkey. In 1920 the city rejected local engineers to ask Boston's Metcalf and Eddy to come up with a flood control program. To carry it out the city hired and then fired its own engineer, Samuel Crecelius, then hired and fired Fort Worth's Hawley and Freese. To finally plan the appearance of the Great Bend as part of a city master plan, in 1929 the city hired, then ignored, Harland Bartholomew and Associates of St. Louis, only to have San Antonio's previously rejected Robert Hugman slip into the breach ten years later—and be dismissed in due course.

With rejection of the plan of Marco Engineering of Los Angeles, the pendulum swung back once again.

Responding to a general outcry against the Marco plan, under the leadership of David Straus the city council and the Chamber of Commerce in 1962 asked the local chapter of the American Institute of Architects for a master plan. A chapter committee chaired by Cyrus Wagner put together a concept for the River Walk, which it named the Paseo del

"Sauerkraut Bend," seen north through the Arsenal Street iron bridge to the old German King William Street neighborhood, was straightened, deepened, lined with concrete and landscaped in the 1950s and 60s.

LEWIS F. FISHER

Most buildings still turned their backs on the River Walk after its construction. These faced South Alamo Street on the future site of the Hilton Palacio del Rio.

Rio. The goal was to create a plan to please San Antonians, rather than a Marco-like concept making the river primarily a tourist attraction. The historic pastoral quality of the river was to mix with commercial activity. The 1963 opening of a riverside Nix Hospital basement room dubbed The Landing as a permanent location for Jim Cullum's Jazz Band was seen as a test of the River Walk's commercial viability.[12]

Zones along the Paseo del Rio were earmarked Quiet, Medium and Loud. Clubs and restaurants were to center in the Navarro Street area of the northern leg of the bend. Along the southern leg were to be quieter entities—antique shops, art galleries, apartment buildings—and on the central leg a mix of restaurants, shops and apartments. Landscaped sections would remain interspersed. To draw crowds and make the project economically feasible, monthly themed fiestas—"Fiesta de Musica," "Fiesta de Bellas Artes," "Fiesta Militar"—would be held.[13]

In April 1963 the AIA chapter's plan was enthusiastically received at Villita Assembly Hall by a crowd of civic leaders, including Mayor Walter McAllister, Chamber of Commerce President James M. Gaines and Atlee B. Ayres, the venerable architect who had advocated a development plan for the river as chairman of a committee fifty-one years before.[14]

City hall named a River Walk Commission with virtual zoning control to carry out a River Walk Ordinance—to keep the "natural beauty and distinctively quaint and romantic character of the river walk area" while tastefully integrating "shopping, entertainment and recreation." Property and business owners formed the Paseo del Rio Association in 1964.

As the River Walk Commission began its work, it faced a nautical problem. In 1949, Casa Rio's Alfred Beyer, taking over Jack White's San Antonio River Company, had replaced rental canoes with two-passenger pontoon paddleboats. Barges fitted with canvas seats were poled by teenagers when not serving as floats in the river parade. Beyer tried building a gondola, but it "sank like a stone." A swan boat like those in Boston's Public Gardens was decapitated by a bridge. A barge designed for dining—the S.S. Enchilada—capsized with diners aboard.[15]

To come up with a river-worthy craft, the River Walk Commission turned to architects Boone Powell and Reginald Roberts, who came up with the now familiar design of flat-bottomed, steel-hulled barges capable of seating up to forty people for sightseeing and twenty for dining.

The new focus on the river was well timed. For in the sort of burst of civic enthusiasm that a half century before sought an improved river as a centerpiece for urban reform, a suddenly ambitious business establishment shaking off twenty years of post-Depression lethargy incorporated a newly defined River Walk into a larger project that would lead to the transformation of downtown San Antonio.

The jump start was to be an event marking the city's upcoming 250th anniversary. This would be nothing less than a world's fair, to open on April 1, 1968—within a few weeks of the anniversary of the founding of the Mission San Antonio de Valero and the presidio of San Antonio de Bexar. Keying off San Antonio's central location in the western hemisphere, its theme would be the Confluence of Cultures in the Americas, and its name would be HemisFair '68.

In July of 1963, ninety-two acres immediately southeast of central downtown San Antonio were chosen as the HemisFair site. Not only did the proposed convention center complex on the site become eligible for urban renewal funds, its western boundary was practically across the street from the midsection of the Paseo del Rio. Plans to energize the River Walk could piggy back on the frenetic planning for HemisFair.[16]

With vital funding for HemisFair and River Walk improvements approved six months later, the Paseo del Rio was extended into the fairgrounds for a third of a mile, ending in a lagoon surrounded by the convention center and its theater. There was a new arched bridge south of Market Street and another over the HemisFair River Walk extension.[17]

The most difficult deadline was assumed by construction magnate H.B. Zachry, who took charge of a critical twenty-one-story, 481-room hotel project on South Alamo Street, facing the fairgrounds and backing

The Hilton Palacio del Rio was completed just in time for HemisFair '68, with one side facing the fairgrounds and the new Convention Center and the other the River Walk. The HemisFair river extension begins at the bridge at left.

Trees give the River Walk hotel La Mansion del Rio, in the original 1852 St. Mary's University buildings, a sense of seclusion.

up on the River Walk. He completed the Hilton Palacio del Rio in short order by using cranes to lift into place modular rooms, assembled off-site and furnished down to towels on the racks and soap in the soap dishes.[18]

Upstream on the northern leg of the Great Bend, another major hotel with the river in its name opened in time for the fair—La Mansion del Rio, centered around the four-story, mansard-roofed stone St. Mary's College building built in 1852 and recently vacated by St. Mary's University's Law School. Renovated and enlarged under St. Mary's alumnus Patrick Kennedy, who pondered the site from above while awaiting the birth of a child in the Nix Hospital, the 200-room La Mansion del Rio surrounded a Mediterranean-style central patio, with a new wing along the edge of the River Walk. During the project the offending 1951 vehicular bridge above the River Walk to Crockett Street was removed.[19]

With two major hotels at distant points on the River Walk guaranteeing a regular flow of pedestrian traffic, space between them became more commercially viable. Building owners began punching doorways in river-level basements as entrances for new shops and restaurants. Near the northeast corner of North Presa and Commerce streets, River Walk activist David Straus built the two-story River Square, opening on the street above and onto a patio below. A fifth pedestrian bridge arching the river was soon added nearby.[20]

A measure of the new respect for the River Walk was the attention from architectural critics during the six months of HemisFair. Ada Louise Huxtable of *The New York Times* spoke for most when she called it "the city's outstanding amenity." River Square was lauded for sensitivity and open space. Austin architect Sinclair Black, writing in the *AIA Journal*, thought La Mansion del Rio's new rear wall beside the River Walk, "neatly folded in response to the giant cypress trees, serves to define the river space and animate its edge. The scale of the magnificent trees becomes more evident by their proximity to the building."[21]

Black used the Palacio del Rio's "conquistador contemporary" design to make a backhanded but "very valuable point about the strength of the river as an urban design context. To have a measure of success, buildings need not be special or particularly well-designed when located on the river. . . . Even a self-conscious attempt inevitably and fortunately fails to dilute the power of the river space."[22]

A transformation rivaling the cumulative efforts of seven earlier decades along the Great Bend had been accomplished in short order, due in no small part, as Hugman and others foresaw, to preservation of its natural beauty. The HemisFair river extension lent promise of unique development to an entirely new area to the east.

Those who engineered the new order of things would have to catch their collective breaths. But soon, along the Great Bend of the San Antonio River and in the corridor beyond, a renewed spurt of evolution would reach heights of attainment then only dimly imagined.

The HemisFair river extension ended in a lagoon surrounded by the new convention center complex, including a theater with a tile mural by Juan O'Gorman. At right is HemisFair's Tower of the Americas.

9. The "Crown Jewel of Texas"

Twenty feet below the street, its noises hushed by the denseness of cypress trees towering above the narrow banks and exotic plants thriving in the sheltered climate, the San Antonio River Walk creates a sense of mystery, anticipation, movement.

Reflected sunlight and shade dance on the rippling water. The muffled clatter of plates delivered to a colorful blur of umbrellad tables mingles with the spicy aroma of the servings, as curving walks—close to the water but rarely with railings—wind around corners and beneath bridges framing new scenes. It is, thought one writer, "a trip through a linear paradise of infinitely changing vistas."[1] The River Walk, noted another, "provides an experience that has not been successfully duplicated anywhere else in America."[2]

San Antonians for more than a hundred years had been saying this could happen. In 1887, one predicted that if its banks were landscaped and its waters traversed by pleasure boats, the San Antonio River could some day become the "crown jewel of Texas."[3]

Sure enough, a century later the San Antonio River Walk became the top tourist attraction in Texas, key to a new $3 billion annual tourism industry in San Antonio and a model for cities throughout the world. In 1995, the American Volkssport Association named a two-hour walk along the downtown river as second in the nation in enjoyment only to a trail along the Hudson River at West Point. A year later the American Society of Civil Engineers named the River Walk and its flood control system a national historic civil engineering landmark.[4]

As the engineers' designation suggests, the San Antonio River Walk has become as much a product of man enhanced by nature as it is a product of nature enhanced by man. The shift is more real than apparent.

Opposite page: Highlighting the River Walk Holiday Festival is the traditional Las Posadas candle-bearing procession, symbolizing the search of Mary and Joseph for shelter, past luminarias at river's edge and beneath trees festooned with lights.

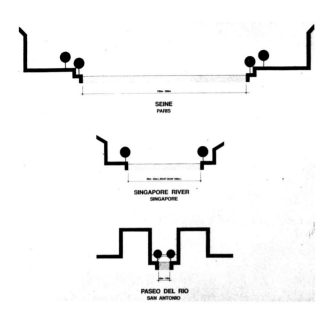

Singapore compared the scale of its river with that of rivers in Paris and San Antonio.

In a system perfected after the close of HemisFair, the San Antonio River's occasional rampages are regulated by a sophisticated but unobtrusive array of dams, tunnels and carefully engineered channels. One set of pumps keeps water at a closely regulated level, while other hidden pumps keep it flowing fast enough along the River Walk to remain fresh. San Antonio River Authority technicians monitor the water's quality. Botanists maintain exotic plantings. Architects and engineers design extensions to bring its waters into new neighborhoods.

Equally unobtrusive are the boards and commissions that govern its development and debate its design, and the thirty-four Parks Department employees assigned to its care. Screened from view are marinas housing the armada of passenger and dining barges, park rangers' patrol boats and maintenance barges used to skim debris from the river's surface in the early morning.

The challenge of replicating the River Walk elsewhere draws a steady stream of inquisitive delegations to San Antonio. A group from Indianapolis returned to lower the White River fourteen feet through the center of its city. Back to Virginia went planners of the $34 million Richmond Riverfront, fifteen feet below street level along abandoned Civil War-era stone-lined canals and locks. "We were incredibly impressed," said the chairman of the Miami River Revival Committee as he returned to Florida to promote a $500 million river project.

Others came from Sacramento, Phoenix, Minneapolis, Kansas City, Louisville, Charlotte, Oklahoma City and elsewhere. From Hull, Quebec, came Canadians planning a French village along their new Brewery Creek River Walk, while from South America came planners from Lima, Peru. In Mexico, Monterrey pumped water back into its long dry Rio Santa Lucía and planted cypresses beside sidewalks lined with tiers of new buildings. "It's supposed to be just like San Antonio," said a Monterrey official.[5]

From Japan have come delegations from Tokyo, Nagasaki, Sapporo and a half-dozen other cities. From China came a group from Suzhou, from Malaysia one planning a $3.5 billion taming of the River Gombak in

Kuala Lumpur. Singapore's Urban Redevelopment Authority sought to put the Singapore River in perspective by studying two river developments "very different but both strongly tied into their communities"—along the Seine in Paris and the Paseo del Rio in San Antonio.[6]

Yet due to the gradual, small-scale evolution along its banks since Spanish times, San Antonio's river seems certain to remain unique despite the intense scrutiny. Citizens and planners have guarded the pace of development since the world rushed in with HemisFair in 1968. Suddenly aware of the heightened danger of unbridled development on the river, city officials turned once more for an overview to a national firm, San Francisco's Skidmore, Owings and Merrill. The planners studied issues ranging from flood control and water quality to housing and social services along an eight-mile river corridor.

At the same time, businessmen and city government closed ranks to publicize San Antonio's new momentum. Capitalizing on a new direction in tourist interest, in 1970 the Greater San Antonio Chamber of Commerce changed its logo to a flowing design suggesting the river, and tourism promoters launched a new campaign: "Forget the Alamo!" In 1973 a gate midway in the cutoff channel was moved south to a new marina and maintenance facility at Nueva Street, enabling tour boats to circle the Great Bend. Improvements financed in bond issues in the 1980s included a parking garage on Commerce street inside the bend.

City officials began actively promoting tourism and conventions. Under City Manager Tom Huebner and the staff he recruited, and assisted by Jimmy Gause, the senior Chamber of Commerce staff member in charge of River Walk affairs, new developers were lured to the River Walk. In 1979 the first major post-HemisFair hotel, the 500-room Marriott Riverwalk, became a visual terminus for the River Walk's HemisFair extension where it turned toward the Convention Center.

Also in 1979, the sixteen-story Hyatt Regency Hotel was begun at the northeast corner of the Great Bend. Planning in 1963 had suggested link-

In Mexico, Monterrey patterned its river walk after San Antonio's.

Linking the river with the Alamo, an extension through the Hyatt Regency Hotel with acequia- and aqueduct-like structures and fountains symbolizes San Antonio's Spanish irrigation system.

ing the River Walk with the Alamo, built as a mission near a spring flowing into the Great Bend. San Antonio's Ford, Powell and Carson was commissioned to design the Paseo del Alamo and create an extension of the Great Bend into the Hyatt's atrium. Water was pumped up to street level a block east, where removing two buildings brought the Alamo into full view. Water flows back down through fountains and acequia- and aqueduct-like structures and channels symbolizing the Spanish irrigation system that gave birth to the city.[7]

"Just add water" was the slogan for the $200 million, ten-acre, million-square-feet Rivercenter Mall when it opened downtown in 1988 on a new branch of the HemisFair river extension. Facing the extension, the three-level mall's 135 shops and restaurants and Imax theater were wrapped in glass—in subtle, blue-based colors—around the new lagoon. A bridge reached an island platform in mid-lagoon for musical and dramatic performances. Beside the mall rose San Antonio's new tallest building, the thousand-room, forty-two-story Marriott Rivercenter Hotel. A tower of similar size was planned nearby, which would make Marriott's river-oriented hotel complex the largest in the Southwest.[8]

As success of the River Walk drew familiar franchises to Rivercenter's food court, it was only a matter of time before more national names appeared along the Great Bend itself. But the demand for commercial space along the Great Bend was exceeding the supply. For twenty years a succession of hotel chains tried to buy the Casa Rio Restaurant for a hotel site. First came Stouffer, then Holiday Inn, Drury Inn and, finally, Sheraton. Instead, in 1992, Alfred Beyer's heirs expanded the first river-level business.[9]

Two developments created new river-level space by cutting back into banks close to the river having only parking lots at street level. One was South Bank, a three-story cluster of new brick buildings in a late-nineteenth century style upstream from the Hyatt Regency. When South Bank opened in 1995, its River Walk tenants included a Hard Rock Cafe and a County Line barbecue restaurant, later joined by Starbucks Coffee.

A new extension of the river reaches River-center Mall's lagoon with its island stage.

Nearby, in 1996 another cut into a former parking lot produced the five-story, stepped-back Presidio Plaza, anchored by Planet Hollywood.

Drawing people to the River Walk was indeed a problem of the past, as it became a magnet for the seven million tourists drawn to San Antonio each year. By the late 1990s, more than a dozen annual events along the river were coordinated by the 120-member Paseo del Rio Association, which by then had its own director and staff, monthly magazine and 500-member support group, Amigos del Rio.[10]

A typical year begins in January, as the Great Bend's dams are lowered and it is drained for several days of maintenance—giving the opportunity for a Mud Festival to crown a Mud Queen and a Mud King to reign over a Mud Pie Ball, Mud Parade and Mud Dance. The eleventh Mud King and Mud Queen, retired Spurs basketball star George Gervin and City Councilwoman Lynda Billa Burke, ascended to their thrones in 1997 by raising more funds to support Paseo del Rio Association activities

When Rosita Fernandez retired after 26 years of starring in Fiesta Noche del Rio, the bridge she crossed nightly to the stage of the Arneson River Theater (*opposite page*) was named in her honor.

than five other candidates—$39,000 of a total of $50,000. During the river cleaning workers have retrieved tables and chairs from riverside restaurants, dishes, baby carriages, Timex watches—still ticking—and even a wedding band, returned to its rightful owner. Archeologists have taken the chance to search the dry riverbed for relics from the Battle of the Alamo.

Merrymakers cosponsored by the Harp and Shamrock Society each March dump in nontoxic dye to turn the Great Bend a Gaelic green for a St. Patrick's Day parade. On the first Monday night of Fiesta Week in April comes the Texas Cavaliers' Fiesta River Parade, as 200,000 spectators line bridges and fill chairs along the banks. A four-night Mariachi Festival follows.

Each summer the Alamo Kiwanis Club holds its long-running Fiesta Noche del Rio in the Arneson River Theater. Rosita Fernandez, who starred in the musical show for 26 years, was such a favorite that when she retired the bridge over which she made her dramatic entrance to the stage was named Rosita's Bridge. In 1984 the theater was the setting for Bizet's opera "Carmen," jointly produced by the Berlin Opera and the San Antonio Festival. Some actors arrived on stage from boats rounding the corner of the Great Bend during the performance. Music was by the San Antonio Symphony, playing on barges anchored to the front of the stage.

In August, the Scout Canoe Race features fifty teams and two dozen media and corporate teams paddling down the river into the Great Bend. In September comes the one-night Pachanga del Rio, a sampling of cuisine of River Walk restaurants. Later in the month, some 20,000 people attend the three-day Great Country River Festival in the river theater at the same time as the venerable River Art Fair.

The river's most memorable series of events is the River Walk Holiday Festival, beginning the night after Thanksgiving and continuing through New Year's Eve.[11]

San Antonio's St. Patrick's Day Parade is held on the river, which is dyed green each year.

Holiday preparations begin in August, with replacement of 70,000 bulbs in strings removed from riverside trees seven months before. Aiding city workers are Amigos del Rio volunteers, who replace as many as a third of the bulbs during an annual Bulb and Socket Party. In September, four professional tree climbers, two grounds people and electricians begin re-hanging the fifty-foot light strings.

On the Friday night after Thanksgiving, the lights are ceremoniously switched on to begin the televised River Walk Holiday Parade. More than two dozen floats wind downstream past 100,000 spectators. Two nights later, singing groups formed by more than nearly two hundred school, church, business and civic organizations begin nearly four weeks of nightly caroling from boats cruising the Great Bend. Carolers perform each Saturday afternoon in December in the Arneson River Theater, where the Alamo Kiwanis Club presents its Fiesta Navidad del Rio.

Luminaria displays, inspired by those in Santa Fe, line the river. Some 2,000 sand-weighted paper bags hold votive candles for the nighttime Fiesta de las Luminarias during the first three weekends in December.

At Rivercenter Mall, boats portraying vignettes of the Christmas story float into the lagoon for a pageant. On the second Sunday in December, the San Antonio Conservation Society cosponsors the candle-bearing Las Posadas procession from La Mansion del Rio to the Arneson River Theater symbolizing Mary and Joseph's search for shelter. After Christmas, college bands from contestants in the nearby Alamodome's Alamo Bowl hold floating pep rallies. The River Walk Holiday Festival concludes on New Year's Eve with entertainment at Rivercenter and strolling musicians, performers and floating bands along the Great Bend.

A nationally broadcast River Walk entertainment feature is American Public Radio's hour-long "Live From the Landing," performances of Jim Cullum's Jazz Band on the River Walk level of the Hyatt Regency Hotel. First presented in 1989, the show is now heard by an estimated one million listeners on 200 of the network's stations.

Luminarias line the river and lights glow from the trees, as seen beside the hotel La Mansion del Rio, during the annual River Walk Holiday Festival.

Some 200,000 persons each year watch the Texas Cavaliers' nighttime Fiesta River Parade, many from the Arneson River Theater.

As activity increased beyond the imaginings of even the most optimistic river boosters of earlier decades, policies became so detailed by 1989 that the city published a nineteen-page *River Walk Policy Guidelines* to outline requirements for building codes, signage, maintenance, concessions, even portable carts.[12]

Issues once disregarded have taken on new significance. Does title to riverside property stop at the River Walk or extend, as in Spanish times, to the river's edge? Now that the river downtown is once more a navigable stream, does state law no longer permit the city to designate whose boats carry tourists and diners? How much more development can be permitted without ruining the River Walk's park-like setting? How much

New construction along the River Walk includes the South Bank complex, which includes a Hard Rock Cafe. In the background is the 16-story Hyatt Regency Hotel.

noise should current businesses be allowed to make, especially since riverside buildings attract increasing numbers of permanent residents?

Two years of study culminated in 1990 with the River Walk's first noise control regulations. Amplified band music was banned mostly after 10 PM Sundays to Thursdays and after 11 PM Fridays and Saturdays. As new clubs drew crowds of younger San Antonians to mix with more restrained tourists, tighter regulations six years later aimed at keeping noise indoors were enforced by park rangers armed with sound meters.

Immediate noise reduction was one reason cited for the city's decision in a battle among eight companies in 1995 for the city's new ten-year barge contract, worth an estimated $40 million. Yanaguana Cruises emerged victorious with its plan to replace at once the noisy gasoline-powered barges with a new fleet of forty steel-hulled barges, patterned closely after the originals but powered quietly through new technology with more efficient engines and odorless, compressed natural gas. The new barges were named after prominent San Antonio women.[13]

In 1988, a retaining wall of stone arches designed by Robert Hugman long before was built below Crockett Street.

In yet another increasingly debated area—design—controversies were running the gamut from a "dogfight" over Presidio Plaza's Dos Chihuahuas folk art shop's sign—two chihuahuas smoking cigarettes and holding a whiskey bottle—to criticism of a topping of stainless steel tubes and spire for the former National Bank of Commerce building, part of its $40 million renovation into an Adams Mark hotel on a little-used northern section of the River Walk. Both designs were finally modified.[14]

By the late 1990s, planning was under way on a major public project to reinforce the main channel's deteriorating stone-lined walls and to improve the channel with a concrete base, as proposed by Harvey Page in 1912 and, later, by Robert Hugman. Hugman's light-colored limestone work which first jarred so many San Antonians had long before weath-

Near the recently-added retaining wall of Hugman's plan, water from a cascade he designed flows through a flagstone section of the River Walk.

ered into harmony with plantings, softening effects of the new construction as Hugman had tried to explain they would. One stone element cut from his plan was finally built in 1988—a wall of arches on the Great Bend below Crockett Street across from La Mansion del Rio. Some hoped the arches could be opened into a yet unbuilt arcade of shops extending beneath the street into the basement of the old Aztec Theater.[15]

Too, Robert Hugman himself was at last recognized for his work. His first major honor came in 1970, thirty years after his abrupt dismissal from the project he conceived, at a ceremony held by the San Antonio

The Left Bank condominiums on the northern River Walk pointed the way for development beyond the Great Bend. The building downstream at right background was being renovated as an Adams Mark Hotel.

Chapter of the American Institute of Architects. "When we praised Mr. Hugman for his vision and design, he broke down and cried," remembered one architect present. "The rest of us stood and cheered him."[16]

In 1978, two years before his death at the age of 78, Hugman was present as Mayor Lila Cockrell dedicated five bells in his honor in the once empty arches behind the Arneson River Theater stage. Lettering of the sign over Hugman's onetime river-level office was later replaced in his memory, becoming his visible signature on the River Walk project.

The River Walk's success not only brought downtown San Antonio an almost around-the-clock vitality uncommon in other cities, it also attracted more permanent residents who, in turn, helped revive the city's core. Conversion of upper stories along the Great Bend into apartments and condominiums encouraged construction in 1979 of the Left Bank Condominiums on the northern River Walk across from the historic former Ursuline Academy buildings, restored as the Southwest Craft Center.

The new housing signaled the potential for significant riverside development outside the Great Bend. A boost to that potential came from an engineering achievement unthinkable not many decades before.

As the daunting flood control program of the 1920s led to development of the Great Bend and the modern River Walk, so did a later mammoth flood control program presage new development beyond protection of the bend's gates. This was a tunnel 24 feet in diameter and three miles in length, extending beneath downtown San Antonio. It could divert 7,000 cubic feet per second of floodwaters, approximately half of the runoff from a hundred-year flood. Landscaping would enhance features of cascading water at the tunnel's inlet and outlet.

Contractors began work in 1987 for the U.S. Army Corps of Engineers, which paid more than 80 percent of the cost, and for the San Antonio River Authority. Also, plans to widen San Pedro Creek's channel downtown for flood control were scrapped in favor of a one-mile tunnel between Quincy and Guadalupe streets, completed two years later.

The river's "inverted siphon tunnel" starts at the southern edge of Brackenridge Park upstream from Josephine Street, where floodwaters can be diverted to a straight drop into the earth, then down a three-mile conduit 24 feet in diameter and some 140 feet beneath the general path of the river. It ends with an equally abrupt vertical rise at its outlet near Roosevelt Park, at an elevation 35 feet lower than its entrance.

Unlike the channel widening and construction of the Great Bend cutoff decades earlier, the tunnel project occurred underground and out of the public view. Yet as it grew into a ten-year effort costing more than $100 million, it had its own delays, dramas and frustrations.

The "Mole," a 620-ton, laser-guided tunneling machine, placed precast concrete segments which formed rings one foot thick and twenty-four

As River Walk use increased, Bizet's "Carmen," co-sponsored by the San Antonio Festival and the Berlin Opera and starring Chilean mezzo-soprano Victoria Vergara, was performed in the Arneson River Theater in 1984.

The "Mole," a 620-ton, laser-guided boring machine, cut a three-mile tunnel and placed thick rings of concrete to carry the river's floodwaters beneath downtown San Antonio.

feet in diameter as it began boring through the earth from the south. But less than 500 feet into the tunnel, fractured shale formations caved in, dropping fragments larger than the borer could grind. It got stuck 150 feet beneath the Brackenridge High School girls' gym. Workers dug a vertical shaft 900 feet ahead, then tunneled back to reach the Mole from the other side and clear away the fallen shale. The rescue took a year.

As engineers put finishing touches on the tunnel in 1997, it became clear that side benefits could be nearly as important as flood control. Three wells in Brackenridge Park had pumped five million gallons of precious water daily from the Edwards Aquifer to keep water in the river downtown. Now, at the tunnel's outlet, riverwater could be captured and pumped up the tunnel to the inlet, then recirculated down the river. Moreover, as part of a larger municipal water reuse program, wastewater pumped from treatment plants to the inlet could add to the downstream flow. Two of the wells could be shut down altogether, while the third provided fresh water to augment water quality.

By removing the threat of extensive flooding between its inlet and outlet, the new tunnel cleared the way for development closer to the level of the river above. Federal hundred-year flood plain regulations remained in place to limit development too close to the river upstream from the inlet—a section of the river almost entirely in Brackenridge Park—and downstream from the outlet, where plans continued for riverside bicycle and pedestrian trails, part of a project to unify the San Antonio Missions National Historical Park by linking the four Spanish missions built along that part of the life-giving stream.

The part of the river now protected from massive flooding falls into three sections. The historic central section, from Lexington Avenue past downtown to Guenther Street, already had a River Walk. But development at the level of river still could occur only within the gate-protected confines of the Great Bend. Restaurants and other facilities along the River Walk outside the Great Bend could now, however, be as close as eight feet above the normal river level, within reach of walkways and boat landings by stairways.

Near-term development along the section below the existing River Walk, from Guenther Street and the warehouses transformed as the Blue Star arts complex, would be primarily an extension of trails to link the River Walk with the Mission Trails project farther downstream.

Planning was already well along for extensive development on the third section, north from Lexington Avenue to the tunnel inlet at Josephine Street and Brackenridge Park. A ready-made destination was the San Antonio Museum of Art mid-way, in a restored turn-of-the-century brewery complex beside the river.

A $32 million project proposed in 1996 would stabilize the channel and raise the water level farther upstream with a dam at Brooklyn Avenue, preparing the way for boats as well as for trails. Still to be decided was whether boats would move between the new levels through locks or on wheels up inclined faces of the dams, or whether passengers would simply be transferred to new boats on different levels. Architects came up with new concepts for riverside apartment and shopping complexes around extensions of the river.

The twentieth century had dawned full of hope for a rejuvenated San Antonio River. With each decade came new levels of achievement. Concern during the first decade brought the major beautification project of the second. The crisis of a major flood in the third decade led to an even greater beautification project begun in the fourth and finished in the fifth. A commercial development plan in the sixth decade sparked the growth of the seventh and eighth, bringing the fine-tuning, new flood control and geographic expansion of decades nine and ten.

From the vantage point of the potential presented to the twenty-first century, however, all that was but a beginning.

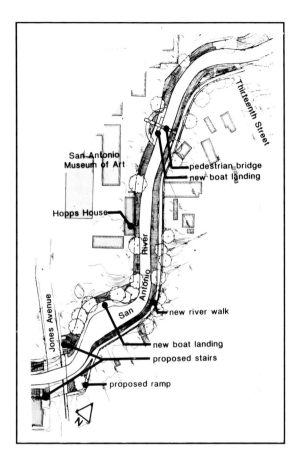

Plans to extend the River Walk northward include a foot bridge and boat landings at the San Antonio Museum of Art, housed in a restored brewery complex.

Chronology

8,000 B.C.— Paleo-Indian hunter-gatherers settle in Olmos Basin and along San Antonio River, called Yanaguana

1535— Explorer Cabeza de Vaca crosses San Antonio River

1691— Headwaters area named for St. Anthony of Padua

1718— Spaniards establish, at first near San Pedro Springs, Mission San Antonio de Valero (the Alamo) and a presidio

1720— Mission San José is first of four Spanish missions established along the river south of San Antonio

1776— Spanish acequia system completed

1819— Devastating flood leaves 16 dead

1842— Commerce Street gets river's first vehicle bridge

1845— Serious flood brings call for dam on Olmos Creek

1849— Polluted river water causes cholera epidemic, 600 die

1865— Serious flood causes three deaths

1869— First municipal flood control effort begins

1871— Houston Street gets river's first iron bridge

1891— New water system drills artesian wells, lowers river

1900— Drought, increased water use first dry up headwaters

1904— Citizens protest cutting trees beside river; city does first riverbank landscaping

1905— First Fiesta river parade

1907— Electric lights decorate river; second river parade

1911— San Antonio River Improvement League formed; artesian well first augments river flow; businessmen commission engineering study of draining and paving the Great Bend

1912— First detailed river beautification plan

1913— River Commissioner George Surkey begins major city river beautification project; two serious floods

1920— Boston's Metcalf & Eddy does river flood control study

1921— Citizens protest cutting trees beside river for flood control; flood devastates city, 50 deaths

1924— City begins major flood control project

1926— Nearly-complete Olmos Dam dedicated; channel straightening and cutoffs, including Great Bend's, begin

1928— City hall rejects plan to drain and pave Great Bend

1929— Losoya Street extension over Great Bend defeated; flood control project completed; Robert Hugman proposes new river beautification plan

1933— City master plan recommends preserving Great Bend without such commercial intrusions as in Hugman plan

1936— Venetian Night revives interest in Hugman plan

1939— Jack White gets WPA to undertake Hugman plan

1941— WPA finishes project; first annual Fiesta river parade

1946— Casa Rio Restaurant is first business on River Walk

1951— River Authority begins extended flood control project

1962— City forms River Walk Commission to oversee growth

1963— City backs architects' plan to revitalize River Walk

1964— Paseo del Rio Association formed

1968— HemisFair, two new hotels energize River Walk; river extended to new Convention Center

1974— First annual Christmas lighting along Great Bend

1979— New surge of hotel, river development begins; Left Bank condominiums reflect increase in riverside housing

1980— City begins River Walk rehabilitation project

1988— Rivercenter Mall opens on a new river extension

1990— Increasing development brings noise control ordinance

1993— New river development studied north of River Walk

1997— Three-mile flood tunnel completed beneath downtown

Notes

1. Water for a Spanish Town

1. This intersection of ecological zones nourishes such a broad variety of plants and animals that one writer termed it "the biological hub" of the northern half of the hemisphere. (W.F. Blair, "Texas Geographic Regions," *TSNL Review* 1(1): 5, 1975, in Karen E. Stothert, *The Archaeology and Early History of the Head of the San Antonio River*, 3.) A section of the basin below Olmos Dam is a State Archaeological Landmark.

2. Stothert, *Archaeology and Early History*, 36, 75. The Indians were observed by C. David Orchard, a longtime amateur archeologist and civil engineer who helped survey the basin for Olmos Dam.

3. The Alamo Madre acequia was begun in 1718 at the Alamo mission's original location, and completed at its final location in 1744. Five feet wide, six feet deep and six miles long, it began at a diversion dam below the river's headwaters and irrigated 900 acres before rejoining the river. Still visible are sections on the Alamo grounds and on HemisFair Plaza.

The Concepción Acequia (1729) began at a dam on the Great Bend near South Presa [Dam] Street and wound south. San José's (1722), the shortest, in at least partial use through the mid-1950s, started north of the mission. One branch irrigated 600 acres the second powered the mission's grist mill. San Juan's began east of San José and has irrigated 500 acres almost continuously since the 1730s. Espada's (1731–45), four and a half miles long, has been in virtually continuous use ever since.

The four-mile San Pedro Acequia (1738), used until 1906, flowed southerly from San Pedro Springs along the divide between the creek and the river. The Upper Labor Acequia (1776) irrigated 600 acres as it flowed southwesterly from a dam near the river's headwaters. Its restored first fifty yards are now used by waterbirds within Brackenridge Park's San Antonio Zoo.

The first acequias north of the Rio Grande were dug near El Paso in 1682 to sustain the mission settlement at Ysleta.

4. Juan Agustín Morfi, *History of Texas, 1673–1779*, 2 vols. (Albuquerque: Quivera Society, 1935), I, 92.

5. Metcalf & Eddy, "Report to City of San Antonio, Texas," 4–7, 9–11.

6. *San Antonio Express*: "Rise of River and Creeks in July 1819," Sept. 18, 1921, 1-A. An estimated depth of nine feet on Main Plaza was termed "almost incredible" by latter-day engineers, who did agree the floodwaters of 1819 reached "a very remarkable height." (Metcalf & Eddy, "Report to City of San Antonio," 12.)

7. Claude M. Gruener, "Rutherford B. Hayes's Horseback Ride through Texas," *Southwestern Historical Quarterly* 68 (Jan. 1965), 359, in Donald E. Everett, *San Antonio, the Flavor of Its Past*, 4.

2. San Antonio Outgrows Its River

1. Frederick Law Olmsted, *A Journey through Texas* (New York: Dix, Edwards & Co., 1857), 149–150.

2. *San Antonio Ledger*: Jul. 28, 1853; *Express*: "Bathing in the San Antonio River," Jul. 30, 1911, 17; "History of City Long Linked to Winding River," Dec. 31, 1933, 7-C; "Two Are Here Who Crossed This Bridge Long Before the Civil War," Aug. 23, 1936.

3. Ibid.

4. Catherine McDowell, "San Antonio's Mills on the River," 1974, ms. in San Antonio Conservation Society Library; Stothert, *Archaeology and Early History*, 60–68. Water dammed for the Concepción acequia dam powered the 1845 William Small/Nat Lewis Mill at what became known as the Mill Bridge crossing. The five-story stone Laux Mill went up to the north in the 1860s on the future site of the Milam Building, the Alamo Mill in 1871 near Avenue B and Eighth Street and, far downstream near Mission San Juan, the Berg Mill in 1879. Two were built by Carl Guenther: the Lower Mill in 1859 at the site of the present-day Pioneer Flour Mills and, nine years later, the Upper Mill upstream near Arsenal and Washington streets. Near the river's headwaters are apparent ruins of a dam and grist mill near the briefly–inhabited suburb of Avoca, laid out in 1838.

Along nearby San Pedro Creek, Simon Menger's San Antonio Soap Works, established in 1850, boiled lye, acid and suet from butcher shops with creekwater to produce soap.

5. Ibid.; Cecelia Steinfeldt, *San Antonio Was*, 86.

6. *Express*: "Brig. Gen. Rochenbach Returns After Absence of 29 Years and Recalls When San Antonio River Froze," Sept. 11, 1928, 11.

7. *San Antonio Light*: "Fishing for S.A. Pearls," Jul. 12, 1937, 3-A.

8. *Light*: "When Boats Dotted San Antonio River," May 22, 1910, 8; *Express*: "History of City Long Linked," Dec. 31, 1933, 7-C.

9. Ibid.; *Express*: "A Steamboat for San Antonio," Sept. 18, 1883, 4; "Sunday Scenes," Jan. 26, 1903, 2.

10. *Along the San Antonio River*, 21.

11. Crystal Sasse Ragsdale, *The Golden Free Land: The Reminiscences and Letters of Women on an American Frontier* (Austin, 1976), 169, in Steinfeldt, *San Antonio Was*, 222.

12. *Light*: "When Boats Dotted," May 22, 1910, 8; *Express*: "Twenty-Three Bridges," Aug. 19, 1911, 18; "History of City Long Linked," Dec. 31, 1933, 7-C; "Two Are Here," Aug. 23, 1936."

13. *Light*: "When Boats Dotted," May 22, 1910, 8; *Express*: "Twenty-Three Bridges," Aug. 19, 1911, 18; "Bridge Built in 1870 Still in Service," Nov. 4, 1927, 8. In 1885 the iron bridge over Houston Street was replaced and moved to Grand/Jones Avenue, where it remained until replaced by a concrete span more than forty years later.

14. "San Antonio, Texas," *Berlin Bridges and Buildings* (Berlin Iron Bridge Company, East Berlin, Conn., Dec. 1898), 126-128; Victor Darnell, Kensington, Conn., interview with Lewis F. Fisher, Nov. 15, 1996. A typical San Antonio bridge was one hundred feet long with a center roadway thirty feet wide. Eight-foot-wide sidewalks were on either side of the main trusses, which curved to a midpoint height of some fifteen feet. Darnell, an authority on the history of the company, knew of no other such decorative posts made by the company.

Observed the Connecticut manufacturer in the article: "Although we are prone to think of Texas as a partially populated state of cattle raising and agriculture bordering on the wild and woolly ideas of civilization and advancement, nevertheless the people of that vast empire are more advanced in their ideas of what constitutes good bridges than many of her distant neighbors who have never crossed the Mississippi River nor stepped foot within her borders."

15. *Express*: "'Letters-of-Gold Bridge' Moved," Dec. 16, 1925, 8. It is believed to be the last surviving bridge of its design in Texas. (T. Lindsay Baker, *Building the Lone Star*, 273.)

16. Sidney Lanier, "San Antonio de Bexar," in William Corner, *San Antonio de Bexar*, 91.

17. Stothert, *Archaeology and Early History*, 60.

18. Corner, *San Antonio de Bexar*, 137; *Express*: "Rise of River and Creeks in July 1819," Sept. 18, 1921, 1-A; Metcalf & Eddy, "Report to City of San Antonio," 7, 12–13; "Report of G. Schleicher, F. Giraud and V. Considerant," in Metcalf & Eddy, "Report to City of San Antonio," 327–35. Identified as specific culprits were new walls that narrowed the channels of both the river and San Pedro Creek, as well as causeways built into the river to support new bridges and the new stone Concepción acequia diversion dam, which not only blocked floodwaters but slowed the flow upstream and caused mud deposits behind it that raised the level of the river. Others suggested solving the problem at the source by digging a channel westward from the Olmos Creek basin to divert the Olmos floodwaters into Alazan Creek, which bypassed downtown.

19. Ibid.; Corner, *San Antonio de Bexar*, 54, 133, 155; McDowell, "San Antonio's Mills." Previously, no map showed the precise boundaries of the river channel so construction beside the river could be monitored. Nor were encroachments officially challenged or regulated, nor alternate flood channels considered. Boston engineers in 1920 praised the 1865 report as "remarkable for its intelligent grasp of the situation and for the breadth of view shown in the measures recommended." (Metcalf & Eddy, "Report to City," 3, 330–334.)

20. Corner, *San Antonio de Bexar*, 54, 154.

21. Metcalf & Eddy, "Report to City," 334.

22. Corner, *San Antonio de Bexar*, 54.

23. T. Lindsay Baker, *Building the Lone Star*, 219–220; Marilyn McAdams Sibley, *George W. Brackenridge*, 127, 130–132, 140. Ownership of the headwaters was still a painful subject for many. Although granted to the city by the King of Spain, a city council feeling itself land poor sold the headwaters area in 1852 to none other than a city alderman, James R. Sweet, over the strenuous objections of City Engineer Francois Giraud and others. In 1859 the property was sold to a buyer who later paid off his note to the city in inflated Confederate dollars. He resold the property—for hard U.S. currency, in 1869—to the mother of George W. Brackenridge. The lush 280-acre Brackenridge estate was a magnet for visiting celebrities, including former President U.S. Grant. Beside Sweet's home, Brackenridge built a Victorian villa from which he could keep an eye on his water works.

24. *Light*: "The San Antonio River," Aug. 19, 1887, 4; *Express*: "Low Stage of the River Becoming Serious," Aug. 23, 1887, 5.

25. *Express*: "The San Antonio River," Aug. 21, 1887, 5; "The San Antonio River," Aug. 23, 1887, 7.

26. Baker, *Building the Lone Star*, 221. The first Market Street complex made way in 1958 for a small building and park above the river.

27. Sibley, *Brackenridge*, 155; Gómez, *Espada Dam*, 24; *Express*: "San Antonio River Assumes Ancient Importance," Oct. 15, 1905, 17.

28. Sibley, *Brackenridge*, 102, 141–142; Stothert, *Archaeology and Early History*, 70; *Express*: "San Antonio River Assumes Ancient Importance," Oct. 15, 1905, 17.

29. Sibley, *Brackenridge*, 141.

3. A Centerpiece for Urban Reform

1. *Express*: "To Beautify The City's River," Jul. 4, 1900, 5; "Sunday Scenes On The San Antonio River," Jan. 26, 1903, 2.

2. *Express*: "Old Spanish Manner Of Cleaning," Sept. 4, 1904, 11; "San Antonio River Assumes," Oct. 15, 1905, 17.

3. *Express*: "Rivercleaning Gang Ruins Beauty Spots," Aug. 18, 1904; "Citizens Stop Ruin Of Cherished River," Aug. 20, 1904.

4. *Express*: "City May Enjoin Building On River," Jul. 15, 1905, 10.

5. *Light*: "Landing of King Selamat," Apr. 25, 1905, 5; *Express*: "Greatest Carnival in History of Texas," Apr. 25, 1905, 5; "San Antonio River Assumes," Oct. 15, 1905, 17. The king, David J. Woodward, was in a line of kings then designated "Selamat," tamales spelled backwards. Tobin Terrace was apparently named for Fire Chief William G. Tobin, who directed the river's cleaning during beautification efforts in 1904.

6. *Express*: "Memorial Day Fittingly Observed," May 31, 1905, 5.

7. *Express*: "Venetian Carnival Pleases," Apr. 20, 1907, 6.

8. *Light*: "All Are Glad They're Here," Apr. 19, 1910, 1; "Civic Pageant An Object Lesson of Great Southwest," Apr. 19, 1910, 4.

9. *Express*: "Public Wants River To Receive First Attention," Feb. 20, 1910, 3; "Plans For Improving River," Mar. 20, 1910, 1-A; *Light*: "Work Starts To Beautify San Antonio River," Mar. 27, 1910, 26; "River Illumination," Apr. 23, 1910, 5. Also being beautified were the quarter-mile from the northern Navarro to Augusta street bridges, 600 newly terraced feet beside the Ursuline Academy and the area below the new St. Mary's parochial school on St. Mary's Street.

10. *Express*: "Water Rights Settled," Nov. 16, 1911, 16.

11. *Light*: "Beautifying of City According to a Definite Plan," Mar. 12, 1911, 33.

12. Ibid.; *Express*: "Will Improve The River," Sept. 27, 1911, 11.

13. *Light*: "Francis Bowen Suggests," Feb. 27, 1903, 4; "Fought Riot On Bridge," Jun. 26, 1910, 7. Three years earlier Simpson formed the San Antonio Canoe Club to paddle cedar-framed, canvas-covered canoes six miles from Brackenridge Park to the Aresnal Street bridge. (*Express*: "Canoe Fleet Will Voyage Down River," Sept. 20, 1908, 24.)

14. W.E. Simpson, "Report On The Design Of A Conduit" in Metcalf & Eddy, "Report to City of San Antonio," 143-150.

15. John A. Booth and David R. Johnson in *The Politics of San Antonio*, 12–13; *Express*: "Final Rally Of Advocates Of New Charter," Feb. 4, 1911.

16. William H. Wilson, *The City Beautiful Movement* (Baltimore and London: The Johns Hopkins University Press, 1989), 1–5, 302–305. By the turn of the century, many middle- and upper-middle-class Americans thought the ideal city an ordered whole in which "dignified, co-operative citizens of whatever station or calling" moved in beautiful surroundings, which, in turn, enhanced worker productivity, improving the economy. A properly appointed modern city needed a stately civic center, parks and boulevard systems. Streets needed to be paved, billboards restrained, trees planted, playgrounds established. But the municipal bond issues these required could usually only be achieved, as in the case of San Antonio, through political reform.

17. *Express*: "Citizens Pitch Their Campaign," Oct. 19, 1910, 1; "Final Rally Of Advocates Of New Charter," Feb. 4, 1911; "Mayor Gus Jones' Death Shocks City," Apr. 8, 1913, 1.

18. *Express*: "Commission Charter Defeated By 168 Majority," Feb. 5, 1911, 1; "Returns Are Canvassed By City Council," Feb. 7, 1911, 18.

19. *Express*: "Start Pump Saturday," Oct. 6, 1911, 11; "Snags Will Be Removed," Oct. 8, 1911, 10-A; "Billboard Men Complain," Oct. 14, 1911, 16; "Ordinance Is Criticised," Dec. 25, 1911, 16; "Coliseum Site and Ground Plan," May 4, 1913, 5-B; "Workers Are For City Federation," May 27, 1913, 9; "Clean-Up Pictures," Jun. 7, 1913, 20; Pompeo Coppini, *From Dawn to Sunset*, 176–177; Harland Bartholomew and Associates, "A Comprehensive City Plan for San Antonio," 225.

20. *Express*: "Start the Big Idea in San Antonio," Feb. 5, 1911, 1-A; "The Big Idea Has Become a Conviction in the Big City That Wants the Bond Issue," May 18, 1913, 1-A.

21. *Express*: "Public Baths One Of The Important Factors In The Campaign For Civic Improvements," Aug. 6, 1911, 15; "Will Improve The River," Sept. 27, 1911, 11.

22. *Express*: "Pump Will Be Installed," Sept. 30, 1911, 16; "City Employees Will Receive Their Pay," Oct. 3, 1911, 5; "For Improving The River," Dec. 29, 1911, 14.

23. *Express*: "Start Pump Saturday," Oct. 6, 1911, 11; "Water Pumped In River," Oct. 9, 1911, 12; "Million Gallons Pumped," Oct. 12, 1911, 13; "River Is Slowly Rising," Oct. 14, 1911, 16; "River Is Underground," Oct. 18, 1911, 5.

24. *Express*: "Irrigation Ditches Dry Before," Oct. 22, 1911, 39-B.

25. *Express*: "City Employees Will Receive," Oct. 3, 1911, 5; "Mayor Is Willing To Dredge River" Oct. 24, 1911, 5; "For Improving The River," Dec. 29, 1911, 14; "For Clearing The River," Feb. 12, 1912, 12; "Rates For A New Light Contract," Feb. 20, 1912, 7.

26. *Express*: "Make City Beautiful Says Mayor," Sept. 1, 1912, 1.

27. Ibid.

28. *Express*: "Free Bath House And Beautified River First Work," Sept. 2, 1912, 1.

29. *Express*: "Plan To Change San Antonio To Big Palm Garden," Sept. 6, 1912, 14; "San Antonio River As It Would Appear If Improved According To Page Plan," Sept. 8, 1912, 1.

30. Ibid.

31. Wilson, *The City Beautiful Movement*, 260; *Express*: "Council Provides For Third Relief," Sept. 4, 1912, 16; "To Write Parts Of New Charter," Sept. 7, 1912, 16; "Refuse In River Retards Efforts For Cleaner City," Sept. 20, 1912; "To Invite City Planner," Oct. 4, 1912, 7; "Will Raise Fund To Hire Architect For San Antonio," Oct. 19, 1912, 5. Two other leading planners were considered, Frederick Law Olmsted Jr. of Boston and John Nolen of Cambridge, Mass. The committee also consulted Chicago architect Marion West, who was doing work in Galveston. (*Express*: "City Plan Meeting," Jan. 21, 1913, 11.)

32. *Express*: "Surkey Seeks To Restore Rustic Beauty Of River," Jun. 27, 1913, 18; "Building Surkey Seawalls To Beautify And Confine The San Antonio River," Aug. 16, 1913, 16; "Surkey's River Beautiful," May 20, 1915, 25.

33. *Light*: "Bowen's Island Will Be Made A Resort Park," Mar. 22, 1912, 3; *Express*: "Bowen's Island Measure Passed By City Council," Feb. 4, 1913, 9. In return for title to the old riverbed, Ward donated land for widening both South St. Mary's and West Nueva streets, built sidewalks and curbs along both streets and absolved the city from any damages incurred in the process. Bowen's Island was in fact a peninsula, surrounded by the river on three sides and on the fourth by the Concepción acequia and its overflow channel.

34. *Light*: "Sans Souci-Coliseum Stock Sells Rapidly," Apr. 21, 1912; *Express*: "Suggested Canal Shortening River Creates Interest," Oct. 30, 1912, 16; "Coliseum Site and Ground Plan," May 4, 1913, B-5.

35. *Express*: "Shorten The River by Cutting Out Bends And Opening A New, Protected Channel," Oct. 29, 1912, 11.

36. *Express*: "Mayor Gus Jones' Death Shocks City," Apr. 8, 1913, 1; "Faults Of City Pointed Out By Mayor Steves," May 31, 1913, 1.

37. *Express*: "Victory For Brown," May 14, 1913, 1; "Bond Issue Will Not Be Greater Than $3,500,000," May 31, 1913, 1; "Bond Issue For $3,350,000," Jun. 3, 1913, 1; "Surkey Seeks To Restore Rustic Beauty," Jun. 27, 1913, 18; "Building Surkey Seawalls," Aug. 16, 1913, 16. Commerce Street, the city's main commercial artery, was losing business to the wider, parallel Houston Street to the north. It was widened by shearing off fronts of buildings facing the street to the south.

38. *Light*: "A Fortune Spent in Rebuilding Commerce Street," Nov. 19, 1914, 15; *Express*: "Dig Up Many Old Relics," Jul. 5, 1914, 3-B; Fisher, *Saving San Antonio*, 69–70.

39. Ibid.; *Light*: "It Will Be Called the 'Jones Bridge,'" Nov. 19, 1914, 16; Coppini, *From Dawn to Sunset*, 205. Sides of the empty northern alcove were later removed for entrances to stairs down to the river. The iron Commerce Street bridge was reassembled downstream to cross Johnson Street. During river widening a half century later, it was dismantled, as was the Sheridan Street bridge, and placed in storage. But workmen sent to scrap the Sheridan Street bridge scrapped the Commerce Street bridge instead, destroying all but one spire and a few fragments. The footbridge now crossing Johnson Street has the surviving spire and three new duplicates. (Carolyn Peterson, "Letter to the Editor," *San Antonio Conservation Society News*, Nov. 1994.)

40. *Express*: "Commerce Street Is Dedicated" Nov. 22, 1914, 4-B.

41. Coppini, *From Dawn to Sunset*, 204; Booth and Johnson in *The Politics of San Antonio*, 13–14; *Express*: "San Pedro Park Has Water Again," Aug. 18, 1913, 12; "Spring Is Flowing," Aug. 26, 1913, 5.

42. *Express*: "To Build River Promenade," Jul. 11, 1915, 1-A.

4. Six Floods in Nine Years

1. *Express*: "Flood Brings Swift Death ," Oct. 3, 1912, 1–2.

2. *Express*: "To Prevent Future Floods," Oct. 3, 1913, 5; "Loss Small," Dec. 5, 1913, 1; "The Reason Today's Express Is Printed on Pink Paper," Dec. 6, 1913, 1; "Today's Express," Dec. 7, 1913, 1; "Gray Is Coming To Investigate River," *Express*, Dec. 7, 1913, 1.

3. *Express*: "Walls Pierced By Openings Would Safeguard City," Dec. 9, 1913, 1; "Flush Gates Are Closed," Dec. 11, 1913, 5; "Expert's Report Shows Olmos Dam The Only Safety," Dec. 10, 1913, 1; "Not A Doubt Of Safety Of Dam, Says Pancoast," Dec. 12, 1913, 1.

4. *Express*: "Straighten-River Plan Idle Talk," Dec. 7, 1913, 4-B.

5. Ibid.

6. *Express*: "City May Build Retaining Walls," Jun. 12, 1917, 18; "Condemnation Of Soledad Property," Jul. 24, 1917; City Commissioners Minutes, Book B, 467–468, 514.

7. *Express*: "Coliseum Site and Ground Plan," May 4, 1913, B-5; "Fund Raised for Coliseum Site," May 25, 1913, 13; "$3,950,000 Bond Issue Election," Jan. 24, 1919, 1; "Bond Issue Approved," Jul. 26, 1919, 1; "City Designates Auditorium Site," Jun. 1, 1920; Metcalf & Eddy, "Report to City of San Antonio," 62.

8. Metcalf & Eddy, "Report to City of San Antonio," 2–3, 135–137.

9. Ibid., ii, 25, 105.

10. Ibid., ii, 27, 53, 122–134. Of the six cutoffs recommended, four were north of downtown: below Josephine Street, saving 1,200 feet; Ninth Street, 2,450 feet; above McCullough Avenue, 950 feet; and above Navarro Street, the cutoff already planned for Municipal Auditorium, 1,495 feet. South of downtown, a cutoff at Durango Street would save 670 feet and the sixth, above South Alamo Street, would save another 285 feet. Two nearby two dams would be removed and tributary channels modified.

11. Ibid., iii–iv, 4, 42–44, 135; *Light*: "Would Cut Out Big Downtown Bend," Jun. 18, 1920, 11; "River Project To Be Started At Early Date," Nov. 5, 1920, 10.

12. Metcalf & Eddy, "Report to City of San Antonio," 32, 109 61-61a. Also, bridges needed to be reconstructed or replaced, since trestle-style bridges caught flood debris and became dams. Those at angles to the river deflected water and those on piers narrowed the channel.

13. *Express*: "River Will Have Broader Channel," Mar. 13, 1921, 1.

14. *Express*: "City-Wide Protest Greets Plan to Remove River Trees," Apr. 1, 1921, 13.

15. Metcalf & Eddy, "Report to City of San Antonio," ii, iv, 112a.

16. *Express*: "Known Flood Dead 39, Scores Missing," Sept. 11, 1921, 1; "Cleanup And Reconstruction," Sept. 12, 1921, 1) Flood-related deaths in Central and South Texas reached approximately 200.

17. *Express*: "Cleanup And Reconstruction," Sept. 12, 1921, 1; "Streets Will Be Cleared," Sept. 16, 1921, 20; "Property Owners Will Be Asked To Pay," Sept. 17, 1921, 1; "One More Street Open," Sept. 17, 1921, 20; "City Prepares To Resurface 14 Flooded Streets," Sept. 20, 1921, 20; "Emergency Food Distribution Ends," Sept. 22, 1921, 22.

18. *Express*: "Property Owners Will Be Asked," Sept. 17, 1921, 1.

19. Ibid.

20. *Express*: "Retention Dam To Protect City Has Approval," Sept. 22, 1921, 1; "Survey Of Olmos To Be Expedited," Sept. 27, 1921, 7.

5. Save It or Pave It?

1. *Express*: "C.F. Crecelius Recommended," Aug. 24, 1924, 8; *Light*: "American Military Engineers Commend Olmos Dam Work," Oct. 19, 1925, 1. S.F. Crecelius had been consulting on an improvement program in Laredo, and nearby had designed five miles of highways and two dams. Before World War I he directed dam and navigation projects in Missouri, Indiana, West Virginia and Kentucky. He rose to the rank of colonel in the U.S. Army Corps of Engineers during service in France.

2. *Express*: "Olmos Detention Dam," Dec. 12, 1926, 26.

3. *Express*: "'Letters-of-Gold Bridge' Moved," Dec. 16, 1925, 8; "San Antonio, City of Bridges," Feb. 5, 1928, 1-A.

4. *Express*: "Engineer Begins Studying Plans," Sept. 3, 1924, 20; "River Channel Work To Begin," Jan. 9, 1926, 1; "Work Begins On River Channel," Jan. 12, 1926, 4; "2,100-Foot River Bend Eliminated," Jun. 1, 1926, 6; "Two Bends In River Will Be Eliminated," Jun. 8, 1926, 8; "Old Mill Wrecked To Straighten River," Aug. 19, 1926, 5.

5. *Express*: "City Buys River Channel Land," Mar. 16, 1926, 9.

6. *Express*: "Ornamental Fountains Between Every Bridge," Oct. 26, 1924, 2; "River Lighting ," Jun. 9, 1926, 24; "Three Plans For Lighting River," Jun. 16, 1926, 9; "River Lighting," Jul. 3, 1926, 20.

7. *Express*: "Queen's Pageant on River Likely," Nov. 13, 1924, 11. In the first of the four rowboats were Crecelius and Emily Edwards, first president of the newly organized Conservation Society. In another was the society's Chairman of Natural Beauty, Margaret (Mrs. Perry J.) Lewis, who was also president of the Fiesta parade sponsoring Battle of Flowers Association. Contrary to later accounts, the boat trip did not persuade city hall to "save" the river; the final debates on that subject were several years away.

Nor did a puppet show—"The Goose With The Golden Eggs," presented by the society to commissioners two months earlier—have much effect on policies toward the river. Despite latter-day reports, the puppet show was directed not at the river but at the importance of saving all the city's unique aspects, represented by six golden eggs. The river was a subcategory of the egg marked "Beauty." (Fisher, *Saving San Antonio*, 3–8, 183–184.)

8. *Express*: "Monks Lauded As Architects," Apr. 5, 1929, 10; Fisher, *Saving San Antonio*, 187, 209.

9. *Express*: "49 Committees Report Ready," May 15, 1928, 10.

10. *Express*: "River Will Be Lighted," Mar. 25, 1927, 9; "River Lighting Conferences," Jan. 25, 1928, 8; "Walk To Be Built Along River Bank," Jan. 27, 1928, 9; "New River Lights," Feb. 15, 1928, 15; "River Lighting," Mar. 22, 1928, 9; "Flood Lights for Illumination of River Approved," Mar. 24, 1928, 2; "San Antonio Praised For River's Condition," Apr. 6, 1928, 4.

11. *Express*: "$175,000 Voted For New Channel," Jun. 15, 1926, 1.

12. *Express*: "New Channel To Cost $250,000," Jul. 14, 1926, 7; "Flood Channel Waits Crecelius," Jul. 30, 1926, 6; "Overflow Channel Plans Nearly Ready," Jan. 13, 1927, 5; "Flood Channel Plans Discard Proposed Street," Jun. 23, 1927, 22; "Street Will Top Overflow Channel," Jul. 2, 1927, 6; "50 Foot Channel Ample, Crecelius," Oct. 18, 1927, 11; "City Will Rent Channel Lots," Nov. 20, 1927, 11.

13. *Express*: "Flood Channel Plans Discard Proposed Street," Jun. 23, 1927, 22; "Street Will Top Overflow Channel," Jul. 2, 1927, 6; "Mayor Outlines Plans For Comfort Stations," Aug. 9, 1927, 8. Wright added that a public restroom building would be built north of Commerce Street for shoppers. From San Diego, Mayor Tobin sent a sketch showing how such a structure could include a barber shop and a Turkish bath.

14. *Express*: "Section of River Cut-Off to Cost City $100,000," Sept. 27, 1927, 24; "Wider Overflow Channel Sought," Oct. 2, 1927, 8.

15. *Express*: "City Will Not Change Plans," Oct. 11, 1927, 8.

16. *Express*: "50 Foot Channel Adequate," Oct. 18, 1927, 11; "Contract Let," Oct. 20, 1927, 22; "Work On Cut-Off Channel," Jan. 24, 1928, 10; Metcalf & Eddy, "Report to City," 54.

17. *Express*: "Bond Issue For Library," Jan. 17, 1928, 8; "Cut-Off Channel Decision," Jan. 26, 1928, 7; "Channel Width Still Unsettled," Feb. 8, 1928, 10; "Channel Width Will Be 70 Feet," Feb. 9, 1928, 9.

18. *Express*: "Channel Width Will Be 70 Feet," Feb. 9, 1928, 9; *Light*: "Crecelius Job In Air," Feb. 14, 1928, 1; "Resignation Refused By Mayor," Feb. 15, 1928, 1.

19. *Express*: "City Urged To Keep Crecelius," Feb. 14, 1928, 8; "Crecelius Salary Cut $400 Month," Feb. 28, 1928, 6; "Flood Prevention Office To Close," Aug. 31, 1928, 15; "Crecelius Quits," Sept. 1, 1928, 7; "2 Firms Named For City Flood Prevention," Nov. 15, 1928, 10. In budget-cutting the next year the city reconsolidated the flood prevention office with the city engineer's office, eliminating 29 of 30 employees. (*Express*: "200 Employees Of City Fired," May 26, 1929, 2-A.)

20. *Express*: "City Ready to Call for Bids," Aug. 12, 1928, 1-A; "Flood Prevention Work Retarded," Oct. 26, 1928, 6;

21. *Evening News*: "River Bed Would Enrich City," Feb. 15, 1928, 1.

22. Ibid.; *Light*: "River Land To Be Reclaimed," Feb. 15, 1928, 2-A; *Express*: "Big Bend Not To Be Eliminated," Feb. 16, 1928, 9.

23. Ibid.; *Evening News*: "River Bed Would Enrich City," Feb. 15, 1928, 1. In recent decades, city hall has been made the scapegoat for a plan to eliminate the Great Bend. No firm evidence, however, has ever been advanced to support that case, nor has any documentation been offered to further define the "counter-movement."

No mention of eliminating the Great Bend appears in minutes of city commissioners' minutes or of the Federation of Women's Clubs. Conservation Society minutes of the time are missing, but contemporary histories by its members make no reference to such an effort. Its quick success may not have left enough time for the movement to become more formal, leaving those in later days to piece together various conjectures to come up with some explanation of what happened. (Fisher, *Saving San Antonio*, 210–211.)

24. *Express*: "City Buys River Channel Land," Mar. 16, 1926, 9; "Church Built In 1886 Will Be Torn Down," Nov. 5, 1927, 6; "Alamo Widening Project," Dec. 12, 1928, 11. At the east, details were being completed in 1928 to widen South Alamo Street. Through southern La Villita the east-west Nueva Street was already being widened. The tallest building in San Antonio, the new thirty-story Smith-Young Tower—later the Transit Tower and then the Tower Life Building— rose at the west, where a new bridge across the cutoff channel would at last connect Villita Street with Dwyer Avenue.

25. *Express*: "City Commission Promises Extension of Losoya Street," Dec. 12, 1928, 11; "Losoya Extension Ordered By City," Mar. 26, 1929, 22; "Street Will Be Built Over River," Mar. 29, 1929, 28.

26. *Express*: "Street Will Be Built Over River," Mar. 29, 1929, 28; "Losoya Extension Plan Abandoned," Apr. 14, 1929, 1-A.

27. *Light*: "Losoya River St. Killed!" Apr. 12, 1929, 1; *Express*: "Suspended Street Project 'Ditched,'" Apr. 13, 1929, 24; "Losoya Extension Plan Abandoned," Apr. 14, 1929, 1-A.

28. *Light*: "Losoya River St. Killed!," Apr. 12, 1929, 1.

29. *Express*: "Losoya Street Extension to South Alamo at Market Street Arranged," Oct. 4, 1929, 1-C.

30. *Express*: "City Given Right To River Channel," Mar. 10, 1929, 13; "City Will Mark Banks," Apr. 23, 1929, 15.

While an 1837 Texas law generally gave the state title and ability to sell abandoned property, the court ruled the city maintained title to the riverbed, abandoned or not, under its land grant from the King of Spain in 1730.

31. *Express*: "Famous Old Lawyers' Office Building to Be Torn Down," Jan. 20, 1927, 6; "River Wall Extended," Apr. 6, 1927, 9; "Home Firm Given Channel Work," Mar. 20, 1929, 28; "Big Bend Cut-Off Work Under Way," Mar. 30, 1929, 22; "Man Fatally Hurt When Flood Tunnel Of River Caves In," Oct. 3, 1929, 1.

The channel took the site of the 1840 Council House Fight between San Antonians and Comanches and that of the landmark 1859 Greek Revival Market House, already torn down for the widening of Market Street.

32. *Express*: "Mayor Is Opposed To Using More Cement In Lining River Banks," Oct. 20, 1929, 1-A.

33. *Express*: "Wider River Channel From Nueva To Guenther Street Favored," Sept. 10, 1929, 7; "Concrete River Channel Doomed," Oct. 22, 1929, 24; "Channel Project Checks Returned," Oct. 23, 1929, 15; "Plans For River Ready Saturday," Oct. 26, 1929, 24.

34. *Express*: "Wider River Channel," Sept. 10, 1929, 7.

35. Ibid.; *Express*: "City To Condemn Land," Oct. 16, 1928, 28.

36. *Express*: "90-Foot Channel Meets Opposition," Aug. 16, 1928, 6; "New Taxable Values" Mar. 30, 1929, 3-C; "12 Acres On River," Jul. 21, 1929, 1-C; Metcalf & Eddy, "Report to City,"61a-62.

37. *Express*: "Mayor To View Proffered Land," Oct. 3, 1929, 10; "Club Women Fight Cut-Off," Oct. 4, 1929, 28; "Women's Clubs to Oppose Removing River Parkway," Sept. 8, 1929, 1-A; "Wider River Channel," Sept. 10, 1929, 7; "Second Protest Against River Marring Filed," Oct. 5, 1929, 10; City Commission To Decide Swiss Plaza Project," Jan. 21, 1930, 26; "Mrs. W.E. Pyne Federation Head," Feb. 21, 1930, 5; *Light*: "S.A. Clubwomen Unite To Fight River Project," Sept. 8, 1929, 1; "City Accepts Swiss Plaza Plan," Jan. 27, 1930, 1. Commissioners approved the deal when the Federation of Women's Clubs dropped its opposition to such projects long enough to approve Swiss Plaza's proposal as long as the city would not put in a concrete channel. In another land swap, Pioneer Flour Mills donated a strip of land for a wider channel for the city to widen South Alamo Street and replace two wooden railroad bridges with steel ones. (*Express*: "City Will Build Bridges in Return For River Land," Jul. 27, 1929, 6.)

38. *Express*: "Mrs. W.E. Pyne Federation Head," Feb. 21, 1930, 5; "City Starts Big Bend Beautification," Apr. 9, 1930, 13; Bartholomew, "A Comprehensive City Plan for San Antonio," vii.

39. *Express*: "River Flow Jazzed Up," Aug. 6, 1927, 4; "Grass on River Banks Will Be Kept Green," Aug. 16, 1928, 3; "Artists Advised To Paint River," Apr. 6, 1929, 10; Bartholomew, "A Comprehensive City Plan," 326.

6. The Beautification Debate

1. Vernon G. Zunker, *A Dream Come True*, 95, 139.

2. Zunker, *A Dream Come True*, 3.

3. Ibid., 95.

4. Ibid., 95–97.

5. Fisher, *Saving San Antonio*, 187, 193.

6. Ibid., 194; *Express*: "Preliminary Steps Toward Creation Of Miniature 'Old World Street' Along Big Bend," Jun. 29, 1929, 8; *Light*: "Unique S.A. Asset Is Plan," Jun. 30, 1929, pt. 7, 1.

7. *Express*: "Mayor Names Plan Body," Dec. 7, 1928, 10; "Street Lay-out In San Antonio Called Problem," May 26, 1929, 1-A; Fisher, *Saving San Antonio*, 135.

8. *Express*: "Prize City Plan Idea Condemned," Jul. 16, 1929, 28.

9. Ibid.

10. Ibid; *Express*: "City Plan Expert," Jul. 19, 1929, 24.

11. *Express*: "Women's Club Members to Urge City to Hire Landscape Architect To Develop River Beautification," Oct. 18, 1929, 8; "Landscape Architect Employment To Wait," Nov. 16, 1929, 24.

12. Alexander Garvin, *The American City* (New York: McGraw-Hill, 1996), 443.

13. Bartholomew, "A Comprehensive City Plan for San Antonio," 322; *Express*: "City Planner View River Improvement," Dec. 19, 1929, 26; "Planner Studies River Work," Dec. 20, 1929, 15.

14. Bartholomew, "A Comprehensive City Plan," 279–283, 321.

15. Ibid., 322–324.

16. Ibid., 325–328.

17. Mary McMillan Fisher, "San Antonio—The Hoover Era," in *Texas Cities and the Great Depression*, Robert C. Cotner ed. (Austin: The Texas Memorial Museum, 1973), 56–57; Bartholomew, "A Comprehensive City Plan," 225.

18. *Light*: "City Passes Zoning Law," Jan. 27, 1930, 1.

19. *Express*: "Springtime," Mar. 17, 1935, 1-A; "Rock Work Adds

Beauty To Parks," Aug. 4, 1935, 1-A; "Rubiola Backs River Program,"
Jul. 10, 1935, 16.

20. *Express*: "Beautifying River D.R.T. Objective," Jul. 6, 1935, 5;
"Rubiola Backs," Jul. 10, 1935, 16; "Architect Tells Of River Beauty,"
Oct. 11, 1935, 18; "River Downtown To Be Lighted," Apr. 8, 1936, 16;
"Boats Christened Almo [sic] And Flora," Apr. 21, 1936, 6.

21. *Express*: "Venetian Night Attracts 10,000," Apr. 22, 1936, 3.

22. Ibid; *Express*: "Dam And Cutoff Control Deluge," Jun. 14, 1935,
1. Jack White had risen from assistant manager of the Gunter Hotel to
manager of the new Robert E. Lee Hotel and left San Antonio to run
the Dallas Hilton. He returned in 1927 to manage the new Plaza, got
active in civic affairs and was elected mayor in 1949. (*Express*:
"Widely Known Hotel Man," Jan. 23, 1927, 4-D.)
The Spanish Revival–style Plaza later became the Granada Homes
for the elderly.

23. *Express*: "Extensive Beautification of Property Along The San
Antonio River Proposed," Apr. 24, 1938, 7-A.

24. Ibid.

25. *Express*: "City Rejects River Plans," Apr. 28, 1938, 10-B.

26. *Express*: "Funds Raised to Put Over River Project," May 22,
1938, 1-C; "Bonds Approved For River Work," Oct. 26, 1938, 1; *The
New York Times*: "San Antonio Dresses Up," May 12, 1940, 7-XX.

27. *Express*: "Triple Check in River Project," Dec. 16, 1938, 8;
Fisher, *Saving San Antonio*, 195.
Maverick got interested, according to the story told his son by Louis
Lipscomb, when the congressman and his friend Lipscomb went down
from the street to the river one night to relieve themselves. Maverick
slipped and fell in. "Louis," he said as he pulled himself out, "we've
got to do something about this river." (Maury Maverick Jr. to Lewis F.
Fisher, interview, Sept. 22, 1996.) The story is sometimes told as
having occurred when Maury Sr. was mayor and Lipscomb was his
police commissioner, an incorrect time to have inspired funding since
by then the river was already funded and the project was well under
way.

7. Transforming the Great Bend

1. *Express*: "Ceremony Starts $265,000 River Beautification
Project," Mar. 25, 1939, 10-A.

2. *Express*: Oct. 30, 1938, 1-A; Zunker, *A Dream Come True*, 133.

3. *Light*: "River Project Being Pushed," Apr. 2, 1939, 4-B; Zunker, *A
Dream Come True*, 145, 167–171.

4. *Express*: "Trees Being Preserved," Jun. 14, 1939, 10; "City To
Place 11,734 Trees Along River," Sept. 17, 1939, 1-A.

5. Robert H.H. Hugman to Mrs. Rena M. Green, Feb. 1, 1940, letter
copy in San Antonio Conservation Society Library; *Express*: "Trees
Being Preserved," Jun. 14, 1939, 10; Zunker, *A Dream Come True*, 155.

6. *Express*: "Rubiola Backs River Program," Jul. 10, 1935, 16;
Zunker, *A Dream Come True*, 158.

7. Zunker, *A Dream Come True*, 119, 148; Fisher, *Saving San
Antonio*; 193.

8. *Express*: "Business Group Looks Ahead To $5,000,000 River
Street," Oct. 30, 1938, 1-A; "Trees Being Preserved," Jun. 14, 1939, 10;
"Water Fills River Bend," Dec. 24, 1939, 1-A; *The New York Times*:
"San Antonio Dresses Up," May 12, 1940, 7-XX; Zunker, *A Dream
Come True*, 166.

9. Zunker, *A Dream Come True*, 144.

10. *Express*: "Trees Being Preserved," Jun. 14, 1939, 10.

11. *Express*: "Water Fills River Bend," Dec. 24, 1939, 1-A.

12. *Light*: "Rock Work On River Rapped," Dec. 21, 1939, 13-A;
Fisher, *Saving San Antonio*, 196.

13. Hugman to Green, Jan. 31, 1940, letter copy in SACS Library.

14. Atlee B. Ayres to Mrs. Rena M. Green, Feb. 1, 1940, letter copy
in SACS Library.

15. *Express*: "Buenz to Boss River Project," Mar. 22, 1940, 8.

16. Maury Maverick to Mrs. Rena Maverick Green, Feb. 19, 1940,
in Fisher, *Saving San Antonio*, 197.

17. *Express*: "Buenz to Boss River Project," Mar. 22, 1940, 8;
Zunker, *A Dream Come True*, 116.

18. *Light*: "Architect May Fight City Discharge," Mar. 22, 1940, 14-
A.

19. Zunker, *A Dream Come True*, 116.

20. *Express*: "Buenz to Boss River Project," Mar. 22, 1940, 8.

21. Fisher, *Saving San Antonio*, 207, 348.

22. *Express*: "River Beautification Project Turned Over to City by
WPA," Mar. 14, 1941, 1-A; Zunker, *A Dream Come True*, 120.

23. Graham, *History of the Texas Cavaliers*, 53–56.

24. Ibid; *Express*: "50,000 See Fiesta Open Despite Rain," Apr. 21,
1941, 1.

25. Graham, *History of the Texas Cavaliers*, 57–58.

26. *The New York Times*: "Gondolas For Texans," Feb. 12, 1939, 1-
XX.

8. From Hugman to HemisFair

1. *Light*: "Glamour Out In War Bond Sales Talk," Apr. 19, 1943, 2.;

2. Louise Lomax, *San Antonio's River*, xxvi. The festival/jubilee typically began as people descended stairs to nine themed sections, with appropriate foods, costumed workers and decorated boats anchored along the banks. In early evening, boats headed downstream as participants followed in a procession along the River Walk to the Arneson River Theater, then formed a mummers' parade onward to a Carnival of Nations downstream. In 1947 the event moved up to the more centrally arranged La Villita, where as A Night In Old San Antonio it draws 100,000 people during four nights each Fiesta and has become the nation's largest single fund-raising event for historic preservation. (Fisher, *Saving San Antonio*, 221–223.)

3. Despite vigorous Conservation Society protests and picketing, the bridge was built in 1951 between St. Mary's and Navarro streets to give the St. Mary's University Law School's new parking garage rear access to Crockett Street. Hugman's office was in the lowest level of the turreted Clifford Building.

4. *Express*: "S.A.'s Casa Rio renewed at 46," Oct. 16, 1992, 7-C; *Express Images*: "Keepers Of The Flame," Sept. 29, 1996, 4–5; Zunker, *A Dream Come True*, 150; Bill Lyons to Lewis F. Fisher, interview Nov. 27, 1996. At first the restaurant was indoors. Then a raised outdoor patio was built, then tables beneath umbrellas were added along the River Walk itself. Gas-fed tiki torches added an exotic touch at night along the walk across the river. To draw attention from the street, the restaurant's name was painted on the upper wall, and two torches blazed behind the sculpture of the Indian on the Commerce Street bridge above.

5. Seth D. Breeding, *Flood Of September 1946 At San Antonio, Tex.*, 1, 8–9, 18. The 1946 storm was centered ten miles southeast of the one that produced the 1921 flood, but the greater intensity of the 1946 rains made the severe runoff of the two storms comparable. (Ibid., 3–4.)

6. San Antonio River Authority, *San Antonio River Authority 1937-1987*, 1, 3, 5, 8. The River Authority, first named the San Antonio River Canal and Conservancy District, was formed under the leadership of Col. W.B. Tuttle—who planned the Fiesta river parade in 1907—in one last, unsuccessful effort to plan straightening and deepening the entire San Antonio River as a barge canal to the Texas coast.

7. Ibid., 9; Fisher, *Saving San Antonio*, 276, 317.

8. Mary Carolyn Hollers George, *O'Neil Ford, Architect*, 157;

Zunker, *A Dream Come True*, 149; Fisher, *Saving San Antonio*, 263-4, 298. By coincidence, two of Rosita Fernandez's uncles had helped build the River Walk's WPA stone bridges.

9. *Express*: "River Bend Park Plan Studied," Oct. 1, 1961, 1.

10. Ibid.

11. George, *O'Neil Ford, Architect*, 157–158.

12. *Express*: "River Bend is Renamed Paseo del Rio," Apr. 16, 1963, 8-B; Boone Powell to Lewis F. Fisher, interview Nov. 23, 1996.

13. Ibid.; George, *O'Neil Ford*, 158. In addition to Wagner, architects on the committee were O'Neil Ford, Brooks Martin, Arthur Mathis, Ed Mok, Allison Peery, Boone Powell, Tom Pressly and Ignacio Torres.

14. *Express*: "River Bend is Renamed," Apr. 16, 1963, 8-B.

15. *Express*: "Keepers of the Flame," *Images*, Sept. 29, 1996, 4; Lomax, *San Antonio's River*, 83–84.

16. *Express*: "Downtown HemisFair '68 Site Picked," Jul. 4, 1963, 1. Of the two other sites under final consideration, one was owned by developer Ray Ellison on the southwestern fringe of the city and the other was along the still undeveloped northern channel of the San Antonio River in a declining region north of Municipal Auditorium.

17. *Express*: "All Seven Bond Isues Carry Every Precinct," Jan. 29, 1964, 1; Fisher, *Saving San Antonio*, 300.

18. Fisher, *Saving San Antonio*, 313.

19. *North San Antonio Times*: Nov. 14, 1981; Fisher, *Saving San Antonio*, 313.

20. At street level, River Square opened onto North Presa Street with a stairway to a River Walk courtyard below, where Arthur P. "Hap" Veltman Jr. was spearheading river development, Street-level facades of adjacent landmark buildings were restored and their rear walls replaced with brick facades opening onto the same courtyard.

21. *The New York Times*: "HemisFair, Opening Tomorrow, Isn't Texas-Size, But It's Fun," Apr. 5, 1968, 49; "San Antonio's Linear Paradise, *AIA Journal*, July 1979, 36.

22. "San Antonio's Linear Paradise," *AIA Journal*, 36. The much vaunted extension of the river into the fairgrounds did not escape unscathed. Its concrete-walled passage beneath South Alamo Street emerged past landscaped terraces inaccessible to pedestrians, making an *Architectural Forum* writer think that "boating through this exten-sion of the Paseo del Rio seems like being under the ramparts of the Morro Castle." (Roger Montgomery, "HemisFair '68, Prologue To Renewal," *Architectural Forum*, October 1968, 88.)

9. The "Crown Jewel of Texas"

1. "San Antonio's Linear Paradise," *AIA Journal*, July 1979, 30. The writer was Austin architect Sinclair Black.

2. *An Evaluation of Expansion Opportunities for the Henry B. Gonzalez Convention Center* (Washington, D.C.: Urban Land Institute, 1995), 8.

3. See pp. 14–15.

4. San Antonio's other national civil engineering landmarks are El Camino Real—the King's Highway—and the acequia system.

5. *Express*: "Richmond likes Riverfront plan," Dec. 8, 1993, 1-D; *San Antonio Business Journal*: "River Walk now serves as model," Apr. 19, 1996, 14; "Monterrey adding Alamo City touch," Sept. 20, 1996, 1.

6. Ibid.; *Singapore River Development Plan* (Singapore: Urban Redevelopment Authority, 1992), 10.

7. Lead architect on the project was Boone Powell. Elsewhere, the Holiday Inn Riverwalk soon went up outside the Great Bend's northern entrance; the Holiday Inn Riverwalk North was built north of Municipal Auditorium as El Tropicano in 1962. A Travelodge was built just south of the southern entrance, and, beyond, a Sumner Suites.

8. "Downtown Renaissance Looks to Retail 'Eden' on the Riverwalk," *Texas Architect*, Sept.–Oct. 1988, 9; "Just add water," *Architectural Record*, March 1989, 100.
Mayor Henry Cisneros and City Manager Tom Huebner helped attract the mall, first planned in 1980 by Edward J. DeBartolo Corp. and Allied Stores and creating 3,000 jobs. Restaurants were kept at river level. To the rear was a 3,100-car parking garage. Work involving water at Rivercenter was designed by Ford, Powell and Carson Inc., the mall by Urban Design Group and Communications Arts of Tulsa, Okla. and the Marriott Rivercenter by Baltimore's RTKL Inc.

9. *Express*: "S.A.'s Casa Rio renewed at 46," Oct. 16, 1992, 7-C. A Baskin & Robbins ice cream outlet opened in River Square in 1980. An Eckerd's Drug Store opened later across the river.

10. A 1995 study showed that of the 6.9 million visitors to San Antonio in 1994, the most—82 percent, or 5.6 million—visited the River Walk and 27.5 percent showed the River Walk to be the single most important reason for their visit, more than three times the number as listing the top attraction the city's traditional top sight, the Alamo, which a less detailed study the same year for the Texas Department of Commerce's Tourism Division showed outranked the River Walk as the state's top tourist attraction. State tourism officials conceded the River Walk's premier rank. (*Express*: "Study says S.A. tourism robust," Oct. 13, 1995, 1; Sarah Temlinson to Lewis F. Fisher, interview, Jan. 29, 1997.)

11. Reflecting the gradual evolution of River Walk events, the Cavaliers' River Parade was first held annually in 1941; the River Art Show, 1947; Fiesta Noche del Rio, 1957; St. Patrick's Day Parade, 1969; Scout Canoe Race, 1970; Great Country River Festival, 1972; Las Posadas along the river, 1973; Mariachi Festival and annual Christmas lighting of the Great Bend, 1974; River Walk Holiday Parade 1982; Mud Festival, 1987; Fiesta Navidad del Rio, 1996. Short-lived events included a New Orleans style Carnival.

12. After thirty years of operating independently, the River Walk Commission was combined with the Fine Arts Commission and the Historic Review Board in 1992 to become the Historic Design and Review Board, dealing with citywide issues. With its oversight diluted at the very time River Walk issues were becoming more intensely debated, many San Antonians began advocating that the River Walk Commission be recreated to preserve a specific focus on the river.

13. *Express*: "River panel OKs holiday festival plan, Sept. 18, 1990; "O'Malley barge group sinks rival," Mar. 10, 1995, 1; "Noise muzzled on River Walk," Jun. 1, 1996, 1.

14. *Express*: "Gallery's sign unleashes River Walk dogfight," Apr. 4, 1996, 1-B; "Hotel redesign," May 7, 1996, 1-B.

15. Fisher, *Saving San Antonio*, 439. The San Antonio Conservation Society contributed $150,000 to help match a federal Economic Development Administration grant for the project.

16. Boone Powell to Lewis F. Fisher, interview Nov. 23, 1996. Honored at the event for re-energizing River Walk development were Walter Mathis, first chairman of the River Walk Commission; Jimmy Gause, senior Chamber of Commerce staff member in charge of River Walk affairs; and River Walk activists and developers David Straus and James L. Hayne, who was instrumental in restoration and development of the Chandler Building on the river at Crockett Street.

Selected Bibliography

Baker, T. Lindsay. *Building the Lone Star*. College Station: Texas A&M University Press, 1986.

Bartholomew, Harland, and Associates. "A Comprehensive City Plan for San Antonio." St. Louis, 1933.

Black, Sinclair. "San Antonio's Linear Paradise." *AIA Journal*, July 1979: 30–38.

Breeding, Seth D. *Flood Of September 1946 At San Antonio, Tex*. Circular 32. Washington: U.S. Geological Survey, November, 1948.

Burkhalter, Lois W., painted by Caroline Shelton. *San Antonio: The Wayward River*. San Antonio: Trinity University Press for Paseo del Rio Association, 1979.

Corner, William. *San Antonio de Bexar*. San Antonio: Bainbridge & Corner, 1890.

Everett, Donald E. *San Antonio: The Flavor of its Past, 1845–1898*. San Antonio: Trinity University Press, 1975.

Fisher, Lewis F. *Saving San Antonio: The Precarious Preservation of a Heritage*. Lubbock: Texas Tech University Press, 1996.

Frary, I.T. "The River of San Antonio." *Architectural Record* 45, April 1919: 380–381.

Glick, Thomas F. *The Old World Background of the Irrigation System of San Antonio, Texas*. Southwestern Studies, Monograph No. 35. El Paso: The University of Texas at El Paso, 1972.

Gómez, Arthur R. *Espada Dam, A Preliminary Historical Report*. San Antonio: San Antonio Missions National Historical Park, 1990.

Guerra, Mary Ann Noonan. *The San Antonio River*. San Antonio: The Alamo Press, 1987.

Gunn, Clare A., and David J. Reed and Robert E. Couch. "Cultural Benefits From Metropolitan River Recreation—San Antonio Prototype." Technical Report No. 43. College Station: Texas Water Resources Institute, Texas A&M University, June 1972.

Lomax, Louise, *San Antonio's River*. San Antonio: The Naylor Company, 1948.

Metcalf & Eddy. "Report to City of San Antonio, Texas, upon Flood Prevention." Boston, 1920.

Minor, Joseph E., and Malcolm L. Steinberg. *The Acequias of San Antonio*. San Antonio: San Antonio Branch of the Texas Section of the American Society of Civil Engineers, 1968.

Ramsdell, Charles. *San Antonio: A Historical and Pictorial Guide*. Austin: University of Texas Press, 1959.

San Antonio, City of, and San Antonio River Authority. "Conceptual Plan for the San Antonio River from Nueva Street to U.S. Highway 281." San Antonio, 1993.

San Antonio River Authority. *San Antonio River Authority 1937–1987*. San Antonio, 1988.

Sibley, Marilyn McAdams. *George W. Brackenridge, Maverick Philanthropist*. Austin and London: University of Texas Press, 1973.

Skidmore, Owings & Merrill, Marshall Kaplan, Gans, and Kahn. "San Antonio River Corridor." San Francisco, 1973.

Steinfeldt, Cecelia. *Art for History's Sake: The Texas Collection of the Witte Museum*. San Antonio: The Texas State Historical Association for the Witte Museum, 1993.

_____. *San Antonio Was: Seen Through a Magic Lantern*. San Antonio: San Antonio Museum Association, 1978.

Stothert, Karen E. *The Archaeology and Early History of the Head of the San Antonio River*. Southern Texas Archaelogical Association Special Publication Number Five and Incarnate Word College Archaeology Series Number Three. San Antonio: Southern Texas Archaeological Association in cooperation with Incarnate Word College, 1989.

Workers of the Writers' Program of the Work Projects Administration in the State of Texas, comp. *Along the San Antonio River*. American Guide Series. San Antonio: City of San Antonio, 1941.

Zunker, Vernon G. *A Dream Come True: Robert Hugman and San Antonio's River Walk*. San Antonio: n.p., 1994, rev. ed.

Index